Second Grade Science

For Homeschool or Extra Practice

By Thomas Bell

Home School Brew Press

www.HomeSchoolBrew.com

© 2014. All Rights Reserved.

Cover Image © sparkmom - Fotolia

Table of Contents

About Us 5
Physical Science #1: Measuring Objects 6
    Types of Scientific Data 6
    Units of Measurement 7
    Tools for Measurement 10
    Activities 12
    Quiz 17
    Quiz Answers 18
Physical Science #2: Motion and Magnets 19
    Laws of Motion 20
    What Is Magnetism? 21
    How Do Magnets Behave? 21
    Activities 22
    Quiz 27
    Quiz Answers 28
Life Science #1: Reproduction and Genetics 29
    What Is Reproduction? 29
    Why Is Variety Important? 29
    What Is Adapting? 30
    What Are Mutations? 30
    What's A Trait? 31
    Activities 32
    Quiz 39
    Quiz Answers 40
Life Science #2: Life cycles 41
    Insects 42
    Activities 45
    Quiz 50
    Quiz Answers 51
Life Cycle #3: Plant Development 52
    Activities 55

Quiz	61
Quiz Answers	62
Earth Science #1: Rocks	**64**
Sedimentary Rock	64
Metamorphic Rock	64
Igneous Rock	64
Special Types of Rock Formations	66
Activities	68
Quiz	72
Quiz Answers	73
Earth Science #2: Soil	**74**
Activities	77
Quiz	81
Quiz Answers	82
Earth Science #3: Environmental or Natural Resources	**83**
Activities	87
Quiz	93
Quiz Answers	94
Earth Science #4: Fossils	**95**
Cast Fossils	95
Mold Fossils	96
Carbon Film Fossils	96
Trace Fossils	96
Activities	98
Quiz	104
Quiz Answers	105

Disclaimer

This book was developed for parents and students of no particular state; while it is based on common core standards, it is always best to check with your state board to see what will be included on testing.

About Us

Homeschool Brew was started for one simple reason: to make affordable Homeschooling books! When we began looking into homeschooling our own children, we were astonished at the cost of curriculum. Nobody ever said homeschool was easy, but we didn't know that the cost to get materials would leave us broke.

We began partnering with educators and parents to start producing the same kind of quality content that you expect in expensive books...but at a price anyone can afford.

We are still in our infancy stages, but we will be adding more books every month. We value your feedback, so if you have any comments about what you like or how we can do better, then please let us know!

To add your name to our mailing list, go here: http://www.homeschoolbrew.com/mailing-list.html

Physical Science #1: Measuring Objects

Objects can be described based on physical characteristics like size, shape, color, or texture. These are very simple forms of measurement. Objects can be grouped together or separated based on certain characteristics as well. In science, objects can be measured using tools like a ruler or a scale to provide more detail on the properties of the object. For example, a rock can be described using words (or qualitatively) as being smooth, gray, circular, and flat. To be specific, you could weigh the rock on a scale to know its mass, or measure the length of the rock using a ruler. In this section, you will explore more about measurements, the different types of measurement or data that can be recorded and simple science instruments that can be used to measure objects.

Types of Scientific Data

There are two main categories of scientific data: qualitative and quantitative.

If you refer to the word *quality*, this will help you remember what qualitative data is. Qualitative data is based on using words, or your five senses (sight, taste, hearing, touch, and smell) to describe an object. Take the animals below, for example, you could describe these animals qualitatively.

What could you say about these animals, using just words to describe the animals' size (big versus small), shape, fur/skin color, fur/skin texture, living environment, method of movement, etc. You might qualitatively describe the animals using some of the statements below:

- The dog is bigger than the hamster
- The frogs are yellow and blue and have slimy skin
- The snake is green, thin, and long
- The rabbit is tan, with large ears, and a soft fur coat
- The parrot has green and yellow feathers, but the other bird is smaller and has orange feathers

The key to qualitative data is that it is what can be observed with your five senses. This type of data does not use numbers or units of measurement like ounces, pounds, meters, inches, or liters.

Quantitative data, on the other hand, refers to the word *quantity*, or the number or amount of something. This type of data involves using numbers and units of measurement to describe the characteristics of objects. You may use statements like, "there are 5 more blue flowers than red flowers", or "the bowling ball weighs 3 pounds". Quantitative data is very important in science and there are several different scientific tools that can be used to measure objects and get detailed information about the quantity or amount related to an object. What types of quantitative statements could you make based on the animals picture on the previous page?

You might quantitatively describe the animals using some of the statements below:

- There are 2 frogs, 1 snake, and 1 rabbit
- The rabbit weighs 5 pounds
- The dog, the hamster, and the cat all have 4 legs
- The fish live in a bowl with 20 cups of water
- The snake is 3 feet long from head to tail

Now that we have discussed the types of data that can be collected, let's look at the types of quantitative measurements that calculated in science.

Units of Measurement

Length

Length can refer to the height or the width of an object. How long is it? In science, scientists generally measure length in meters, using a meter stick. However, in the United States, we often use inches or feet to measure the length of objects. A table may be 48 inches (4 feet) long, or your height may be 60 inches (5 feet). Length can also be described as distance or the length of travel from start to finish. We often travel long distances that to use inches or feet would be a very large number. Larger units for length like yards or miles can be used. The scientific unit for distance is the kilometer, however, we often use miles to describe distance. A marathon is 26.2 miles, whereas a football field is approximately 120 yards (which is equal to 360 feet). Understanding what you are trying to measure will help you determine the appropriate unit of measurement to use. Let's look at a few images and discuss the unit of measurement for length that would be best.

What units should be used to measure the car? You could probably use inches, but that would be a lot of counting. Instead, you would measure the car in feet. How about the cellphone? This is a smaller object in comparison to the car, so inches would work just fine for this object. Let's know look at weight.

Weight

Weight can be measured in several different units. Scientists use grams or kilograms to measure the weight of objects. In the United States, pounds or ounces are used to describe the weight of objects. For example, when you were born, you may have weighed 8 pounds and 4 ounces. The pounds and ounces help to define your weight. If you were to measure an ant, you would have to use a much smaller unit for weight. A single ant would not weigh a pound or anything near that amount, but we could measure an ant in a smaller unit called a gram. A gram is 0.002 pounds, or you could say that 1 pound is 454 grams. That's a lot of grams for one pound! An ant may weigh 0.001 grams, which is a very small number. For very large objects, like an elephant, pounds are too small of a unit for weight. You could use pounds, but the weight of an elephant in pounds is approximately 15,000 pounds. That's a lot of pounds! Instead, you might use tons for the unit of measurement. One ton is equal to 2,000 pounds. The weight of an adult male elephant is approximately 7.5 tons! Look at the images below and try to predict what unit of measurement would be best to measure the weight of the object.

What weight unit would be the best for the rocking chair? The rocking chair is not extremely small, so grams would not be the best unit. The rocking chair is not as large as the truck and could be lifted by an adult. So, using pounds may be okay for the rocking chair. What about the truck? This is a large object that is not easily lifted, so tons would be the better unit for its weight. Let's now look at how we measure liquids.

Volume

We can use even more units of measurements to measure the volume (or amount) of a liquid. What units of measurement have you heard of in relationship to liquids? We may buy a *gallon* of milk, or a recipe may call for a *cup* of milk, or a tomato sauce can may have 64 *ounces* of tomatoes, and even still you may buy a 2 *liter* bottle of soda. Like with the other units of measurements, the one you use depends on the amount and size of the liquid you are trying to measure. Scientists generally use liters for volume, however, in the United States, we often use liters, cups, or ounces. What volume unit would be best for the images below?

Other Units of Measurement

We may measure other things like: time and temperature. Time can be measured in years, months, weeks, days, hours, minutes, or seconds. Temperature can be measured in Fahrenheit (in the United States) or in degrees Celsius. The weather report is a great example of how temperature is measured. The meteorologist may comment that, "today's high temperature will be 75°F".

Tools for Measurement

Now that we have discussed the types of measurements and the units of measurement, let's look at the scientific tools or instruments that can be used to determine these measurements.

For length, we can use a simple ruler, a meter stick, a yard stick, or even measuring tape. Depending on the distance or length you are trying to measure will determine which of these instruments is best to use.

For weight, we often use a scale or balance. This can be seen in the doctor's office which records your weight or in the grocery store when your parents weigh the fruit before they buy it. Some scales are extremely sensitive and are able to record very, very small weights, like the weight of an ant. Whereas other scales are very large and able to record large weights like tons.

For volume, you can use a beaker or graduated cylinder similar to the images below. Measuring cups or measuring spoons can also be used, especially when measuring volumes or amounts for recipes.

For time you may use a calendar, a clock, or even a stopwatch. Depending on the amount of time you are trying to measure will determine if a calendar (for longer periods of time) is better to use than a stopwatch (for shorter periods of time).

For temperature, we use thermometers. These can be in degrees Celsius or Fahrenheit. Some thermometers have both units, with Celsius on one side, and Fahrenheit on the other.

Classifying objects using qualitative and quantitative data is an important part of science. As you can see, there are lots of measurements we can take and even more types of scientific tools we can use to calculate those measurements.

Activities

#1 - Sliding is fun!

Note: For this experiment, you will want to have at least 3 people.

Materials:

- Flat surface with an edge, like a table or desk
- Deck of cards
- Paper
- Pencil
- Ruler

Procedure:

1. Divide the deck of cards evenly among the number of people that are present. For example, if there are 4 people, then each person will get 13 cards.
2. Place the card on the flat surface. One at a time, have each person place one finger on the card and flick or slide it forward toward the edge of the flat surface. The goal of this step is to slide the card far enough that it is as close as possible to the edge of the flat surface as possible.
3. Use a ruler to measure the length of the distance between the cards and the edge of the table/desk. You can use millimeters, centimeters, or inches, but it is important to use the same measurement each time.
4. Have each person go one at a time, repeating steps 2 and 3. Who slid their card the farthest?

What's happening?

Usually sliding cards across a table does not seem like a learning activity, but when math and measurement are involved, it can be! In this experiment you were able to practice measuring lengths and using a ruler.

#2- Jump, Jump, Jump Around

Note: For this experiment, you will need a partner.

Materials:

- One liquid crystal thermometer
- Stopwatch, or a watch that shows seconds
- Paper
- Pencil

Procedure:

1. Write a two-column chart; one column should state "resting" and the other should state "after exercise."
2. Have one person first sit down and hold a thermometer to their foreheads for approximately one minute.
3. After the minute is over, look at the temperature and record it on the paper.
4. Have the person get up and run in place or do jumping jacks for two minutes without resting.
5. When the two minutes are up, take their temperatures again. Write this number down on the paper.
6. Subtract the resting temperature from the after-exercise temperature. The remaining difference is how many degrees higher your temperature rose after exercising.

What's happening?

When you exercise, you probably feel hotter and begin to sweat. This experiment shows that you feel hotter and sweat because your temperature actually does rise when you exercise. We can determine the change in temperatures by subtracting the two temperatures.

#3: Who needs a ruler?

Materials:

- Metal paper clips (at least 50 of them)
- Paper and pencil
- Household objects (spoons, shoes, socks, tie, etc)

Procedure:

1. Find several objects around your house. Some should be short and some should be long.
2. Estimate how many paper clips will be needed to measure the object.
3. Line the paper clips one by one along the object and see how many paper clips are needed to measure it. Was your estimate close?
4. You can link the paper clips together to create a paper clip measuring tool.

What's happening?

Other objects besides a ruler can be used to measure items. It is always good practice to make estimates and then use tools to test if your estimates were accurate. In this activity, you were able to explore with measuring items with paper clips. A paper clip is about an inch long, so really, you made your own flexible, growing ruler!

#4: The Mystery Box

Note: This activity works best with two people. One person should know what the object is, while the other person has to guess.

Materials:

- Shoebox with lid
- Small object (this should be able to fit in the showbox)
- Duct or MaskingTape (optional)

Procedure:

1. Place the object in the box.
2. Put the lid on the box. You may choose to tap it closed, if needed.
3. Give the closed box to the other person and ask them to figure out what is in the box. They cannot open the box, but they can shake the box.

   Be sure to listen to the object in the box as it is shaken. Does it sound like it rolls? Is it heavy? Does it move around a lot in the box?

   4.) After 5 minutes reveal what is in the box.

What's happening?

Since you cannot see the object in the box, you have to use your senses and make qualitative observations of the object. Based on how it sounded as it moved in the box, helps you determine certain characteristics of the object. It's not easy to figure out what the object is without knowing what it looks like, but with this activity you explored tapping into your other senses to help you solve the mystery.

#5: You're How Old?

Note: This is best done with at least two people.

Materials:

- Tree
- Flexible measuring tape

Procedure:

1. Find a tree.
2. Wrap the measuring tape around the trunk of the tree. Be sure you choose the widest part of the tree to measure.
3. Read the measurement in inches.
4. The number of inches is equal to the age of the tree. For example, a tree that is 40 inches around would be 40 years old!

What's happening?

Trees are a type of plant. Each year they grow a new layer of bark to protect themselves, growing about an inch wider every year. For a tree that has been cut down, you can count the rings on the tree stump from the center to the outer edge and this will also tell you the age of the tree. A tree makes a new ring every year when it grows a new layer of bark.

Quiz

Check Your Understanding

1.) What are the two types of scientific data?
2.) _____ data involves observations.
3.) _____ data involves numbers.
4.) True or False. Qualitative data involves your five senses.
5.) True or False. A ruler can be used to measure the volume of a liquid.
6.) Name three scientific instruments that can be used to measure length or distance.
7.) A football field should be measured with a _____.
8.) Name a unit for distance.
9.) Name a unit for weight.
10.) True or False. A beaker can be used to weigh an object.
11.) What weight unit is used for very tiny objects that have small weights?
12.) An elephant is best measured using _____.
13.) 2,000 pounds is equal to _____.
14.) Name three units of measurement for volume.
15.) Scientists use _____ to measure volume.
16.) Name one scientific instrument that can be used to measure the volume of a liquid.
17.) _____ and Fahrenheit are the two units used for measuring temperature.
18.) What scientific instrument is used to calculate the outside temperature?
19.) _____ can be used to measure time like how long it takes to run around the track.
20.) True or False. A calendar can be used to measure long periods of time.

Quiz Answers

1.) The two types of scientific data is qualitative and quantitative.
2.) Qualitative data involves observations.
3.) Quantitative data involves numbers.
4.) True. Qualitative data involves your five senses. These are observation statements that do not involve calculations or numbers.
5.) False. A ruler can be used to measure distances, especially short distances.
6.) The ruler, the meter stick, and the yard stick can all be used to measure length or distance.
7.) A football field should be measured with a yard stick. You could measure it with a ruler, it would just take a lot longer.
8.) The meter is a unit for distance. Other answers can include: inches, feet, miles, and/or kilometer.
9.) The pound is a unit for weigh. Other answers can include: grams, kilograms, tons, and/or ounces.
10.) False. A scale can be used to weigh an object. A beaker is used to determine the volume of a liquid.
11.) The gram is used for very tiny objects that have small weights like an ant.
12.) An elephant is best measured using tons. Remember tons are very large weight units for objects that are not easily picked up.
13.) 2,000 pounds is equal to one ton.
14.) Liter, ounces, cup are units of measurement for volume.
15.) Scientists use liters to measure volume.
16.) A beaker or a graduated cylinder can be used to measure the volume of a liquid.
17.) Celsius and Fahrenheit are the two units used for measuring temperature.
18.) A thermometer is used to calculate the outside temperature.
19.) A clock or stopwatch can be used to measure time like how long it takes to run around the track.
20.) True. A calendar can be used to measure long periods of time. This is true if you are measuring the number of days between Christmas and the 4th of July.

Physical Science #2: Motion and Magnets

Motion is all around us and is an important part of physics, a type of science. Some objects may move a lot, while others may not seem to move at all. Take Earth for example, if we are standing still, Earth is actually moving in an orbit around the Sun. Scientists have discovered ways to explain what movement or motion is and how motion can change.

Objects move based on force. In order for an object to move, some type of force has to act on the object to get it to move. For example, a cup will not fly off the table or move without you either picking up the cup or pushing it over. Your hand acts as the force, causing a motion to occur on the cup. Motion can be further described in terms of how fast the motion is. Velocity and speed are terms used by physicists to describe the rate or how quickly, or slowly an object is moving.

What is acceleration? How is that related to motion? Acceleration is how the velocity of an object changes over time. For example, if you are going on vacation and traveling on the highway at a speed of 65 miles per hour, that is your velocity. Note: this means that each hour, you cover a distance of 65 miles. Let's say that your parents are driving and they are able to keep that speed for 2 hours, until they notice a traffic jam ahead. They will likely have to slow down, say to 45 miles per hour. This changes your motion or your velocity. After 1 hour, once you pass the traffic jam, your parents may be able to increase their velocity to 65 miles per hour again. In this example, the velocity decreased, then increased. By knowing how the velocity changed and how long it changed for, you would be able to determine the car's acceleration. If we accelerate in a car that means the velocity is changing and it is increasing. If instead, we decelerate, that means the car is slowing down, so the velocity is changing, but this time it is decreasing.

The mass of an object can influence the motion of the object and the force needed to move the object. Think of it this way...

Is it easier to move a house or a toy block? A house has a large mass or weight and it can move, but you would need a large amount of force to push or pull the house. A toy block is small and has a small mass. This could easily be moved by you pushing it or picking it up.

There are types of motion. Motion can be simple or complex.

Simple motion movements are in a straight line. The object can be slowing down or speeding up, but its motion can be traced or tracked on a straight path. The movement of a bowling ball rolling down a bowling lane would be an example of simple movement.

Complex movements involve direction changes, like when an object is going in a circle, in a random path, or at an angle. When a baseball is hit in the air, its movement would be complex, as the ball travels up, at an angle, and then comes down to the ground.

Laws of Motion

Sir Isaac Newton, an English scientist put forth three principles or laws that applied to motion. These laws are used in physics to describe the movement of objects and how they behave as they move.

Newton's First Law of Motion: An object at rest will stay at rest and an object in motion will stay in motion, unless acted upon by an outside force. Take the bowling ball for example. If you were to place the ball down gently at the beginning of the lane, the ball is not likely to move and travel toward the pin. This is what Newton describes as "an object at rest, will stay at rest", meaning if the object is not moving, it will continue to not move. If we want the bowling ball to travel toward the bowling pins, then we would need to apply a force to move the ball. The force in this example can be your hands pushing or throwing the ball toward the bowling pins.

What about an object that is already moving? According to Newton's law, if an object is moving, it will continue to move forever until some force makes it stop. Take for example when you kick a soccer ball. The ball moves through the air, and Newton says, it will continue to move until something stops it. Well, gravity will pull the ball down toward the ground, but then the ball will begin rolling. The ball will continue to roll, until another force (the ground) makes it stop. The ball may get caught in a water puddle, get tangled in the grass, or get slowed down as it rolls over rocks. The ground in this case is providing a force called friction to make the ball slow down and eventually stop.

Newton's Second Law of Motion: The acceleration (how velocity changes) is related to the strength of the force and inversely related to the object's mass. What does this all mean exactly? Well, this law is saying that the ability to speed up an object or slow down an object depends on two things: the force and the mass of the object. Take a car for example. Cars are heavy or have a high mass, this means, it is harder to change the velocity of a car, unless a great force is applied. Likewise if you have a very light object, it would be easy to change the object's speed and a small amount of force can do so.

Newton's Third Law of Motion: For every action, there is an equal and opposite reaction. This is the idea that forces come in pairs. Think about swimming. As your hand pushes through the water, the water pushes back on your hand. According to Newton, if one force or action is happening in one direction, then there is an equal force or action happening in the opposite direction. As long as the forces are equal then the object does not move. For example, if the water is pushing with a force of 10 Newtons (Note: Newtons is the unit of measurement for force. The larger the number, the larger the force on the object), then your body would be pushing with an equal force of 10 N against the water. If instead, the forces are not equal, let's say there is a large wave in the pool and the water is now pushing against you at a force of 20 N, but your body is still pushing with the same 10 N against the water, the water has the larger force and will be able to move you.

Motion is an important part of the universe and motion can occur when objects are attracted to another and also when objects are repelled. Let's now dive into magnets!

What Is Magnetism?

Magnetism is a type of force that can cause motion. Magnetism is created by electricity. But what causes electricity? Small particles within objects called electrons help to create electricity. Within every object, there are small spheres called atoms. Within an atom is a smaller sphere that is called the nucleus. Around the nucleus are electrons that move in circles or orbits around the nucleus. This is similar to how the Earth moves around the Sun! Electrons have a negative charge and they spin either up or down. In most objects, the number of electrons that spin upward are equal to the number of electrons that spin downward. When this happens they cancel each other out. However, in some objects like iron, the electrons spinning upward are not equal to the electrons spinning toward, and these extra electrons can attract other objects, like metals.

Magnetic objects are all around us! There are even magnetic objects in outer space. The Sun and Earth are very magnetic, because there spins of the electrons are not equal. Deep inside the core of the Earth is a dense ball of iron metal. It is this metal core that allows compasses to work and find North.

There are naturally magnetic rocks called lodestones. For thousands of years, people made magnets using lodestones. It is not clearly understood exactly how lodestone became to be magnetic. Some scientists believe that lodestone became magnetic after having been struck by lightning.

How Do Magnets Behave?

If you have ever experimented with magnets, you may have observed a very peculiar behavior. Magnets have poles or ends. Just like Earth, magnets have a North and South Pole. If you place two magnets together, they can either attract each other, or repel each other. This is where the statement "opposites attract" is important. Magnetics placed together with opposite poles (South and North or North and South) touching will attract each other. On the other hand, magnets with the same pole (North and North or South and South) touching will repel each other.

Magnets can be made using elements found on Earth, like iron, aluminum, nickel, or cobalt.

Activities

Try these fun experiments to learn more about motion and magnets!

#1 – I spy something…magnetic!

Materials:

- 2 large plastic cups or containers
- 4 magnets of different sizes and shapes
- 1 paper plate or flat surface
- 10-15 items such as bouncing balls, plastic toys, metal toys, paper clips, crayons, magnetic pieces, erasers, etc.

Procedure:

1. Label four of the cups with the words "Magnetic" and four of the cups with the words "Not Magnetic".
2. One by one, place each of the items on the paper plate and use each magnet (one at a time) to pick up the object.
3. If the magnet can pick up the object put it in the magnetic cup. If not, put it in the not magnetic cup.

What's happening?

Magnets have an unequal number of spinning electrons. This makes them very attracted to metals. When you place a magnet near something that has metal, the magnet will attract or stick to it. When you place the magnet near something that does not have metal, the metal seems to not do anything and will not stick to the object.

#2 – Magnetic power

Materials:

- 3 plastic containers with lids
- Pipe cleaners (have different sized ones)
- 3 magnets of various sizes and shapes

Procedure

1.) Before starting the experiment, you should cut the pipe cleaners into smaller pieces. You can make them however long or short you like 1 inch pieces work best.
2.) Add the strands into the containers and close the lid. Be sure to keep the different size strands separated.
3.) Place a magnet somewhere on the container (the top is usually best) and slightly shake the entire container.
4.) After the container has been shaken, the pipe cleaner strands should be sticking to the container where the magnet was placed.
5.) Carefully count the number of strands that stuck to the magnet. You may need to take the lid off and count them outside of the container.

What's happening?

Magnets have invisible force fields that make them attracted to metals, just like the metal that is found inside the pipe cleaners. The power, or force, of the magnet is strong enough that it can pass through some materials, like the plastic of the container or lid.

#3: Round and round

Materials:

- Penny
- Balloon

Procedure:

1. Place the penny inside of the balloon. The balloon should NOT be blown up.
2. Carefully blow up the balloon, making sure that the penny stays in the balloon.
3. Tie the balloon closed.
4. With the penny inside of the inflated balloon, begin to move the balloon in a circle. Going faster and faster each time.
5. The penny should begin to travel around the inside of the balloon in a circle.
6. Stop moving the balloon and the penny should keep moving!

What's happening?

The penny was at rest before you started moving the balloon. When you applied a force, moving the balloon in a circle, the penny moved. The penny continued to move even after you stopped moving the balloon until gravity pulled it down. Remember Newton's first law of motion: "An object at rest will stay at rest, and an object in motion will stay in motion, unless acted upon by an outside force."

#4: The Card and the Penny

Materials:

- One playing card
- Small cup (plastic is best)
- A quarter

Procedure:

1. Place the card on top of the cup.
2. Put the quarter on top of the card.
3. Very quickly pull the card straight out from under the coin.

4. Watch what happens to the coin!

What's happening?

The quarter wants to not move, this is called inertia. When the card is moved the inertia is greater than the movement of the card, so the quarter remains in the same spot, even if the card is not there. Without the card, there is nowhere for the quarter to go expect inside of the cup.

#5: Vanishing Colors

Note: This experiment requires **adult supervision.**

Materials:

- Liquid white glue
- 12 inch Ruler
- Pencil
- String
- Scissors
- 4" x 4" piece of cardboard
- Paper plate
- One plastic cup

Procedure:

1. Cut the entire edge off of the paper plate. You should be left with a circle.
2. On the circle, trace the opening of the cup and cut it out.
3. Using the ruler, divide the circle into six equal sections.
4. Color the circle a different color in each section.

5. Trace a circle on the cardboard, using the opening of the cup and cut this circle out.

6. Glue the colored circle to the cardboard.

7. Ask an adult to make two holes in the center of the circle.

8. Lace the string through the two holes and tie the ends of the string together.

9. Move the string in a circular motion to wind it up.

10. Hold the string firmly, one piece in each hand, and pull tight and watch the wheel of colors spin!

11. Where did all the colors go?

What's happening?

The colors on the wheel seemed to disappear. This is because the fast movement of the wheel made all the colors blend together and make it seem as if they were not there at all.

Quiz

Check Your Understanding

1.) _____ is all around us and is an important part of physics.
2.) True or false. Objects move based on force.
3.) What is velocity?
4.) If a car is accelerating, then it is _____.
5.) If a car is decelerating, then it is _____.
6.) True or False. The mass of an object does not influence its motion.
7.) Movement in a curve or random path is called _____ motion.
8.) Movement in a straight path is called _____ motion.
9.) _____ was an English scientist that studied the laws of motion.
10.) True or false. An object in motion will automatically stop.
11.) True or false. An object at rest will stay at rest.
12.) Force is measured in what unit?
13.) Magnetism is created by _____.
14.) Give two examples of magnet objects (not including magnets).
15.) True or false. The quartz rock is a natural magnet.
16.) True or false. Magnetism happens when the number of electrons spinning one way is equal to the number of electrons spinning another way.
17.) The ends of a magnet are called _____.
18.) Opposite _____ of a magnet attract each other.
19.) Identical poles of a magnet _____ each other.
20.) Name an element that can be used to make a magnet.

Quiz Answers

1.) Motion is all around us and is an important part of physics.
2.) True. Objects move based on force. Forces can be you pushing or pulling on an object, but it is needed to cause motion or movement.
3.) Velocity is similar to speed; it is how fast an object is moving.
4.) If a car is accelerating, then it is speeding up.
5.) If a car is decelerating, then it is slowing down.
6.) False. The mass of an object does influence its motion. Think of it this way…the larger the object the harder it will be to move and the more force you will have to apply to move it.
7.) Movement in a curve or random path is called complex motion.
8.) Movement in a straight path is called simple motion.
9.) Sir Isaac Newton was an English scientist that studied the laws of motion.
10.) False. An object in motion will remain in motion unless acted upon by an outside force. Gravity is the force that usually causes objects to stop moving.
11.) True. An object at rest will stay at rest unless acted upon by an outside force. This is Newton's first law of motion.
12.) Force is measured in Newtons or N.
13.) Magnetism is created by electricity (or electrons).
14.) The Earth and the Sun were two examples of natural magnets mentioned in the section.
15.) False. The lodestone rock is a natural magnet.
16.) False. Magnetism happens when the number of electrons spinning one way is not equal to the number of electrons spinning another way. If the numbers are equal, the electrons "cancel" themselves out. With magnets all of the electrons are not canceled out.
17.) The ends of a magnet are called poles.
18.) Opposite poles of magnets attract each other. Like if you were to put the South pole of one magnet near the North pole of another magnet, they would attract or come together.
19.) Identical poles of magnets repel each other.
20.) Iron, aluminum, nickel, or cobalt are elements that can be used to make magnets.

Life Science #1: Reproduction and Genetics

Life can be a mysterious process. How exactly is life formed? In this section we will go through some of the basics of reproduction and how traits are inherited or passed on from one generation to the next. At the end of this section you will have the opportunity to explore inheritance much more with some activities that involve studying and learning more about your family's traits.

What Is Reproduction?

Reproduction is the process that organisms go through to create new organisms or offspring. There are two different types of reproduction: asexual and sexual.

Asexual Reproduction is when one organism splits into two, forming an exact copy of itself. Humans do not reproduce this way, but bacteria do. This is a very quick and easy process but does not allow for a lot of variety. Think if it this way, if you were to create a copy of yourself and then your copies create more identical copies, there would be a lot of "you" running around. Copies that all look, act, and think the same way.

Sexual Reproduction is when two organisms have to come together and share material. This involves the mating of a male and a female. The male has sperm which carries the important information for the father and the female has eggs that also carry important information but from the mother. The egg and the sperm have to meet and the sperm has to go inside of the egg. When this happens, the sperm's information or DNA and the egg's information or DNA mix together to make a baby that has a mixture of the two pieces of DNA. Now, this is where there can be lots of variety. Based on the information that each parent gives the child will determine how the child looks and what traits the child can have and pass on to their children, when they have them.

Sexual reproduction is not as fast as asexual reproduction because it involves more organisms (2 instead of 1) and after the egg and the sperm meet, the baby has to grow inside of the mother or inside of an egg. For example, you grew inside of your mother's womb for 9 months after the egg and the sperm met and a baby bird has to grow inside of an egg for 2 weeks before it can hatch.

Why Is Variety Important?

In nature, the more variety or differences we have the more likely we can adapt to different things. If everyone were to look and behave the exact same way, what could we really learn from each other? Not much. If all the birds looked the same, ate the same things, and lived in the same area, it would be hard for them to survive as food ran out or space became limited. If the environment should change, it is much harder for identical organisms to live. Even if we all have very little differences, that is still variety. Variety allows us to adapt.

What Is Adapting?

What do you do if you are cold? You may shiver, put on a coat, or get a blanket. You are adapting or trying to deal with the cold temperature. Animals and plants have to adapt all the time. There are some things like the temperature that are outside of our control and all we can do is try to adapt the best way we can. Some animals are able to better adapt than others. The polar bear can live in very cold environments because it has a thick layer of fat that protects it from the cold and keeps warm. Humans don't have this, so we would likely not survive in a very cold environment without having some source of heat, like a fire. Animals are able to adapt based on what traits they have. These traits are passed on from their ancestors and are traits that help the animal to live. Take the giraffe for example its long neck was developed over hundreds of years as they had to stretch farther and farther up into the trees for leaves. Those giraffes that inherited the long neck from their parents were better able to survive until all giraffes had a long neck. In many cases, organisms are different because of mistakes or mutations that happen inside of the organism's body.

What Are Mutations?

Inside of our body we have cells. There are millions of cells in our body and they are responsible for keeping us alive. Inside of our cells is a special structure called the nucleus. The nucleus is like a bank vault, it stores the treasure of the cell which is the DNA. DNA is like a recipe, it has all of the information to know how to make cells, which cells to make, which body parts to make and when, even what we will look like. As cells divide, the DNA has to be copied so that each new cell has their own copy. When the DNA is copied mistakes happen by accident. Think about when you may type or write something and you have a typo. A mutation is like a typo. It is done randomly and in some cases does not affect anything, but in other cases, the mutation may change the entire DNA recipe. Mutations happen all the time, in every organism. Mutations also help to give variety to make sure everyone's DNA recipe is slightly different. Many times mutations can be a helpful thing and can give an organism a new, special trait that helps it to survive better. Let's look at an example.

Roaches are an annoying and gross bug. They can usually be killed with rock spray. If you use rock spray on a roach, it is likely to die, but some may live. Why is that? Some roaches may have a mutation that changed their DNA recipe to allow them to live even if they are sprayed with roach spray. Now, this mutation may not work on every single type of roach spray, but it does help them survive some of the roach sprays. Scientists would say that the roaches have become *resistant* meaning they can resist dying.

We see the same thing in humans. Have you ever had to take antibiotics? Antibiotics are designed to kill bacteria like if you have an ear infection or strep throat. They usually work to kill most bacteria, but sometimes you may get infected with bacteria that are resistant to the antibiotic. This is because the bacteria may have a mutation to allow it to live even if you are taking antibiotics. Like with the roach example, the mutation will not allow the bacteria to resist all antibiotics, so switching to a different antibiotic may kill the bacteria.

These resistances are able to be passed on when the organism reproduces.

What's A Trait?

For this section we will define a trait as a physical characteristic. You may have the trait for blue eyes, or the trait for curly hair. Traits are passed on from generation to generation. Traits that are harmful or make it harder for an organism to live are usually eliminated over time. So, the traits we have should be able to help us survive and adapt to our environment.

What does "passed on" mean?

The traits we have like eye color, skin color, height, hair texture, even diseases are inherited from our parents. This means that the DNA recipe from your mother and the DNA recipe from your father mixed together to create you. Depending on how they mixed together will determine important physical traits about you. Your parents' traits came from the mixture of their parents DNA, just like your children's traits will come from the mixture of your DNA and your future husband or wife's DNA. Some traits are dominant and may occur more often. Brown eyes are an example. Other traits are recessive and in general may not occur more often. Colorblindness is an example of a recessive trait.

Some traits run in families. You may notice that all the members in your family are tall or they all have blond hair. In this case, the trait for tallness runs in your family. When people with different traits have children this creates lots of variety. For example, a man with black hair and brown eyes may have a child with a woman with brown hair and green eyes. They may have a son with black hair and green eyes and a daughter with brown hair and brown eyes. The way the parents DNA and traits mix is completely random, so there are a lot of possible combinations of what traits the children can inherit. It is also possible to have children that have the same physical characteristics as one of the parents. This does not mean that the child is identical to the parent because remember the child's DNA recipe is made from their mother and their father, not just one parent. So, on the outside the child may look like their mother or their father, but if we were to dive into their cells and look at their DNA recipes, they would be different. Identical twins are the only two types of people that will have identical physical characteristics and identical DNA recipes.

Activities

Test out your understanding of traits and inheritance with these eye-opening experiments!

#1: Who Has What?

For this experiment you will need to talk to at least 5 other family members.

Materials:

- Pencil and paper
- 5-8 family members

Procedure:

1. On a piece of paper, make a table with 6 columns and 8 rows.
2. On the far left column write the statements below, one in each box going down the side of the paper.

I have attached earlobes

I can roll my tongue

I have dimples in my cheeks

My hair is naturally curly

I cross my right thumb under my left thumb when I clasp my hands

I have freckles on my skin

I write with my right hand

I have food allergies

3. At the top of the second column, write your name.
4. For each statement, write yes or no in the second column.
5. Find other family members and have them repeat step 4, putting their responses in the other columns.
6. Look at the traits of your family members. Do you all have the same traits? Are there any ones that are different?

What's happening?

Traits are passed on from your parents. Even if you have the same parents as your siblings, you could have inherited different combinations of traits. For example, you could have dimples, attached earlobes and be right handed, but your brother could be left handed. IN nature, there is no one way of inheriting traits, it is done randomly, so the combinations of traits that a child can get from their parents are endless!

#2: Can you taste it?

Materials:

- PTC paper (this can be bought on the internet)
- 5-10 people (can be family members)

Procedure:

1. If the PTC paper is not already cut into strips, cut the paper into long thin strips.
2. Place the paper on your tongue and observe the taste.
3. On your paper mark "yes" if the taste of the paper is bitter or mark "no" if you do not taste anything.

4. Find 5-10 other people, can be family members and repeat steps 1 through 3. Keep track of how many "tasters" and how many "non-tasters" there are.

What's happening?

About 75% of people can taste the bitter taste of the paper, while 25% may not taste anything. The ability to detect the bitter taste is something you inherited from your parents. A scientist discovered that the types and strength of our taste buds depends on what we inherit from our parents.

#3: Who do you look like?

Materials:

- 7 plastic containers
- permanent marker
- Small colored blocks or objects (6 of each color - red, yellow, blue, green)
- Paper and pencil

Procedure:

1. Label each of the container as follows: Grandfather 1, Grandmother 1, Grandfather 2, Grandmother 2, Father, Mother, Child
2. Mix up the colored blocks and without looking choose 6 blocks and put them in the container marked Grandfather 1.
3. Repeat step 2 for the Grandmother 1, Grandfather 2, and Grandmother 2 containers.
4. Write down how many colors are in each container.
5. Without looking choose 3 blocks from Grandfather 1 and place it in the Father container.
6. Without looking choose 3 blocks from Grandmother 1 and place it in the Father container.

7. Write down how the colors and how many of each are in the Father container.

8. Without looking choose 3 blocks from Grandfather 2 and place it in the Mother container.

9. Without looking choose 3 blocks from Grandmother 2 and place it in the Mother container.

10. Write down how the colors and how many of each are in the Mother container.

11. Without looking choose 3 blocks from the Father container and place it in the Child container.

12. Without looking choose 3 blocks from the Mother container and place it in the Child container.

13. Write down how the colors and how many of each are in the Child container. How do the child's blocks compare with their grandparents? Or their parents?

What's happening?

This is how traits are passed on. They are passed on randomly from what is there to choose from. You didn't look when choosing the blocks, so the combinations of blocks likely changed as you went through the experiment. This is how traits change over time and are passed on within our families. In some cases, two people can have the same colored blocks. This is true in real life as well. Sometimes family members can have the same characteristics, like twins or triplets, it's rare, but it happens!

#4: What's inside?

Materials:

- Resealable plastic bag
- Fresh strawberries (3-4 large ones)
- Dish washing detergent
- Measuring spoons

- Salt
- Water
- 2 clear plastic cups
- Filter (a coffee filter works fine)
- Rubbing alcohol
- Wooden stick (popsicle sticks work great!)
- Measuring cup

Procedure:

1. Remove the leaves from the strawberry.
2. Place the strawberries into the plastic bag, seal, and carefully smash them.
3. Measure 2 teaspoons of dish washing detergent and 1 teaspoon of salt and place it in the plastic cup.
4. Measure ½ cup of water and pour it into the plastic cup with the salt and detergent.
5. Take 2 teaspoons of the liquid from the cup and carefully add it to the bag with the mashed strawberries. Reseal the bag.
6. Gently mix the contents in the bag with your fingers. Try not to make too many soap bubbles in this step.
7. Place the paper filter on the empty plastic cup.
8. Pour the strawberry solution through the filter.
9. Pour about ½ cup of rubbing alcohol down the side of the cup over the strawberry solution.
10. Use the wooden stick to scoop up the cloudy white substance that forms on the side of the cup. This is the strawberry's DNA!
11. If it didn't work this time, try it again with one of the other strawberries you have left.

What's happening?

You have found the DNA of the strawberry! DNA is a special part of all living things, this is the "recipe" that tells our bodies how to grow, how they will look and what traits we can pass on to our children. DNA is the most important thing in our body's cells because without it our body would not know how to function. What you pull out on the wooden stick is the important information for the strawberry. This white, cloudy material has all the information on how to grow the strawberry, when to have it ripen, even when it will rot and die.

#5: What color are your eyes?

Note: For this experiment you will need to talk with your grandparents, parents, and siblings. If you cannot talk with your grandparents, ask your parents to help.

Materials:

- Large white poster board
- Pens, pencils and markers (green, gray, blue, brown)

Procedure:

For this experiment you will be tracking the eye colors throughout your family.

1. Make a family tree, similar to the image below, using circles to represent the people.

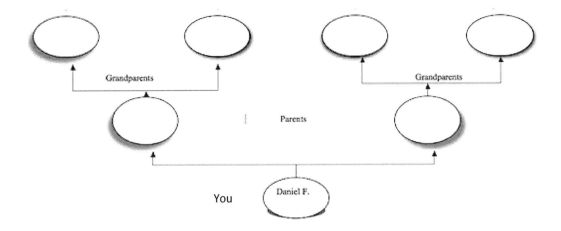

2. Ask each family member what their eye color is and color their circle with that color. If you're able, ask your grandparents about their parents' (your great grandparents) eye color.

3. You should end up with a family tree that has different colors for you to track how the eye color in your family is passed from one generation to the next.

What's happening?

Traits like eye color are passed from your parents to you. You may notice that your whole family has the same eye color or you may see that there are lots of different eye colors in your family. Your eye color is determined by the traits that your mom and your dad have and how they mix together. Since our genes are not always seen by looking at a person, it is not uncommon for two people to have a child that has a different eye color from both of the parents!

Quiz

1.) What are the two types of reproduction?
2.) _____ reproduction is when an organism splits into two organisms, both being identical.
3.) Which type of reproduction happens the fastest?
4.) True or False. Sexual reproduction involves two organisms.
5.) What is inside of the nucleus?
6.) Why is DNA important?
7.) What is the definition of a trait?
8.) How are traits passed on?
9.) What is a mutation?
10.) True or False. A mutation is an intentional change in the DNA recipe.
11.) Why do animals need to adapt?
12.) Give an example of a trait.
13.) Mutations provide _____.
14.) True or False. Having a lot of variety is bad for the population.
15.) Give an example of a recessive trait.
16.) Give an example of a dominant trait.
17.) Which type of trait, dominant or recessive, occurs more often?
18.) _____ have identical copies of DNA.
19.) How can a child and a parent look the same but have different DNA recipes?
20.) When you have children your DNA recipe will mix with what?

Quiz Answers

1.) The two types of reproduction are asexual and sexual reproduction.
2.) Asexual reproduction is when an organism splits into two organisms, both being identical.
3.) Asexual reproduction happens the fastest because one organism can split into two organisms.
4.) True. Sexual reproduction involves two organisms, one male and one female.
5.) The DNA or DNA recipe is inside of the nucleus.
6.) DNA has all the information of how to grow the organism, what they will look like, and what traits they will have.
7.) For this section, we defined a trait as a physical characteristic.
8.) The DNA recipes of the parents is mixed together and this determines what traits are passed on and what traits the child will have.
9.) A mutation is a change in the DNA recipe. This happens when the DNA is copied.
10.) False. A mutation is an accidental change in the DNA recipe. Most mutations are never noticed and some can allow the organism to have a new and helpful trait that it didn't have before.
11.) Animals have to adapt to their environment in order to be able to survive.
12.) Answers may vary. In this section height, skin color, eye color, and hair texture were given as examples of traits.
13.) Mutations provide diversity or variety.
14.) False. Having a lot of variety is good for the population. The more variety the more likely organisms can change and adapt to their environment.
15.) Having colorblindness is an example of a rare and recessive trait.
16.) Brown eye color is an example of a dominant trait.
17.) Generally dominant traits occur more often than recessive traits. There is one important exception. Dwarfism is a dominant trait. So, in this case everyone who is not a dwarf is recessive, meaning dwarfism does not occur very often.
18.) Identical twins have identical copies of DNA.
19.) Physical traits can be the same, but the DNA recipe can be different depending on how the DNA recipes of the person's parents were mixed together.
20.) When you have children your DNA recipe will mix with your husband or wife's DNA recipe to determine what traits your child will have.

Life Science #2: Life cycles

Another characteristic of living things is that they grow and change over time. You can think of how this happens in terms of a life cycle. For plants the cycle goes like this: A seed lands in a place where it can grow—somewhere where it has soil, sunlight, and water—and it germinates, or begins to sprout. It grows small roots; then tiny leaves break through the soil. The plant continues to grow, getting larger and producing more leaves. When it is fully grown, it can produce seeds of its own—often from a flower—and the cycle begins again when the seed is pollinated and drops or is carried from the plant.

Animals go through life cycles too, although the cycle may start in different ways. There are three phases of life for animals: before birth, young, and adult. Let's explore each phase.

Before birth – depending on the animal this phase can take place inside of an egg or inside of the mother's womb. Some babies hatch from eggs. Insects, fish, amphibians, reptiles, and birds (and a few mammals) start out life this way. During this phase, important structures like the brain, the heart, the backbone, and the organs form. Most animals look the same during this phase, since most animals need the same important parts to survive. The time spent in this phase varies greatly depending on how long the mother is pregnant. For a cat, pregnancy lasts about 2 months. For a human, this phase would be about 9 months long, but for an elephant, the mother is pregnant for almost 2 years!

Young – this phase could last 1 day to 18 years. Some animals like the deer or the horse expect their young to be able to walk and run immediately after birth. Whereas monkeys nurture their young for years before letting them leave and live on their own. Bears send the young off to the wild alone after one year with their mother. Many reptiles are expected to find their own way immediately after hatching and will never be nurtured during this phase. During this type, there is rapid growth of the body. Reproductive structures like the ovaries in females and the testes in males will continue to grow but will not be fully developed to have babies.

Adult – this part of life is characterized by being able to reproduce. This is the stage in life when an animal is able to have its own young. For some animals, this stage is not reached for over 10 years, for other animals, this may be reached within 1 year or less. During the adult phase, the animals body may continue to grow though much slower than it did in the young phase. At the end of this phase is death. Though death can be a scary thought, it is a natural part of life. An animal can die in any phase of the life cycle and most animals are more likely to die in the before birth and young phases than any other phase. For the adult animal, especially those entering "old age" their mental and physical abilities begin to break down and they may behave like an animal in a much young phase of life. For example, an older gorilla may not be able to walk as far, which is very similar to the same physical limits of a young gorilla. The life expectancy for an animal varies greatly. Humans have an average life expectancy of about 75 years, an elephant can live for 70 years, a crocodile for 50 years, and a tortoise can live for over 100 years!

Plants and animals live finite lives that may last hours or many years, but they all die. Reproducing ensures that others will take the place of those that die.

Let's look at the life cycle of some interesting animals.

How does life begin for amphibians?

Amphibians, like frogs have a somewhat complex life cycle. Unlike other types of animals, they go through a big change called a metamorphosis. This means that the animal in the young phase will look very different than the animal in the adult phase. Generally amphibians are born either hatching from eggs or from their mother's womb, then they live during the young phase in the water. Since amphibians are able to live on land **and** in the water they have to have gills (for the water) and lungs (to breathe on land). The tricky part is that the gills and the lungs cannot develop at the same time. The gills will develop first, so the young frog or tadpole will spend most of its childhood in the water breathing with gills. As the tadpole grows, it begins to lose some of its body parts like the tail and the gills will be replaced with lungs. As the adult frog, it will now spend most of its life on land.

Scientists say that frogs go through a partial metamorphosis because the young and the adult phases are only slightly different. Let's look at an organism that goes through a complete metamorphosis.

Insects

These creatures are amazing because their young stage looks nothing like their adult stage. They completely change in a very short period of time. We will look at the life cycle of a butterfly.

What are the stages of the lifecycle of a butterfly?

There are four stages for the butterfly's life cycle. They are: the egg, the larva, the pupa, and the adult.

The egg – is the unborn stage. In this stage the eggs are laid by the female butterfly. She will generally lay her eggs on plants. The plants will be the food source for the growing butterfly when it hatches from the egg as the caterpillar.

The female butterfly lays eggs in the every season, except for the winter. The exact egg-laying time depends on the species of butterfly. During each laying, hundreds of eggs are released. Butterfly eggs are very, very small. There is a high chance that most eggs laid will not become butterflies, so the female lays as many eggs as she can in the hopes that at least some will grow, hatch, and survive.

The larva – After the egg has been laid, the next stage is the larva stage. The "baby" emerges from the egg and is called a caterpillar. The main job of the caterpillar is to eat as much as it possibly can. The caterpillar will eat and eat and grow and grow during this stage. The caterpillar will grow so much that it will have to split and shed its skin at least 4 times. As the caterpillar eats the food is stored for it to use in later stages.

Did you know a caterpillar can grow over 100 times bigger than it was when it first hatched? Most caterpillars are the size of a pen tip when they first hatch but can grow to be 2 inches long within the matter of 2 weeks!

The pupa – The caterpillar will enter this stage after it is full grown and has eaten all it can eat. For butterflies the pupa is called a chrysalis. The chrysalis may attach under a branch, bury itself underground, or hide in leaves. Different species of butterflies spend this stage in different ways. During this stage, the cocoon is formed to protect the growing pupa. This stage could last up to a month! Some species are known to be in this stage for two years!

This is when the metamorphosis or the big change occurs. Parts of the pupa will grow very quickly to make the wings, legs, and eyes of the adult butterfly. The stored food from the larva stage will be what the pupa lives off of as it grows inside of the cocoon.

The adult – After all of the growing is done, the butterfly will emerge from the cocoon, completely transformed! The butterfly looks nothing like the egg, or the caterpillar that it came from. The caterpillar is almost blind, with few eyes and has short legs and short antennae. The adult butterfly is the exact opposite. It has many eyes with great sight, long legs and antennae. Butterflies spend their time flying and eating nectar from plants. There are some butterflies that do not eat at all and instead continue to live off of the food they stored as a caterpillar. But, butterflies do not continue to grow! They stay the same size during the adult stage.

In this stage, the butterflies main job is to mate and lay eggs to make new butterflies. The female adult butterflies will fly from branch to branch looking for the right spot to lay her eggs to start the cycle all over again. She has to be sure to find the right spot, so when the eggs hatch they have lots of food nearby.

Butterflies have a very short life span. Most only live two or three weeks. Some butterflies are able to live through the winter by hibernating and these types of butterflies can live for several months.

Do all insects go through a complete metamorphosis?

No. In fact some insects like the grasshopper and cockroaches go through an incomplete metamorphosis. This means that they do not go through the pupa stage and their life cycle is a bit simpler.

These insects have: the unborn stage or the egg, the young stage called the nymph, and the adult stage. During the nymph phase they eat as much as possible and grow very rapidly. In the adult stage the growing slows dramatically, wings form, and the insects main focus becomes mating and laying eggs to start the cycle all over again. Like insects that undergo complete metamorphosis, these insects' life spans are also very short lasting no more than a few months.

Animals are amazing and grow in many different ways. In the next section, you will learn about how plants grow and develop!

Activities

Try these fun science activities to learn more about animal development.

#1 – Wormy becomes a butterfly

Materials:

- Caterpillar (this can be purchased online, if not found outdoors)
- Terrarium with lid
- Plant materials

Procedure

1. Place the plant materials into the terrarium.
2. Carefully add the caterpillar.
3. Be patient and watch as the caterpillar eats and eats and eats for several days.
4. Eventually it will form a chrysalis and emerge as the beautiful butterfly!

What's happening?

The caterpillar moves through the life cycle towards becoming a butterfly. In this case, though, the students actually get to see them transform during each stage.

#2: Growing Fruit Flies

Materials:

- Sliced fruit (apple, banana, and grapes)
- Clear plastic container with plastic lid
- Knife

Procedure:

1. Ask an adult to cut several slits in the plastic lid with the knife.
2. Place the sliced fruit in the container.

3. Let the container sit in a well-lit corner for several days.
4. Voila, you've made fruit flies!

What's happening?

Fruit flies are amazing little creatures. They have special sensors to find the smell of ripened and rotting fruit. They are so small that they can easily creep into your home when they smell fresh fruit nearby. Once they find the rotting fruit, they lays eggs, sometimes on the fruit itself and start to make other fruit flies. If you're not careful, you'll have thousands of fruit flies before you know it! The life cycle of a fruit fly is less than 8 days. They can go from an unhatched egg to full grown adult in about a week's time. Amazing, right?

#3: Here come the maggots!

Materials:

- Plastic container with lid
- Raw fresh meat (steak or beef is best)
- Small plastic container
- Corn meal (optional)

Procedure:

1. Place the raw meat in the large plastic container and seal with the lid.
2. Place the container outside in a sunny area and leave for 1.5 days.
3. Carefully take the lid off and leave it off. This is not the best smell, but it's great to attract flies!
4. Leave the container uncovered and outside for another 1.5 days.
5. After 1.5 days, seal the container and bring it indoors and put in a shady and cool place. You can also leave it outside in a shady place where animals won't disturb it like an outdoor window sill.

6. Wait for a few days and maggots should start to hatch in the container on the raw, decaying meat.

7. If you transfer the maggots to the small plastic container and give them corn meal, they will eat and eat and eat and then form the pupa, just like a caterpillar forms the chrysalis.

What's happening?

When the meat is outdoors covered it begins to decompose from the heat of the sun. When it is left uncovered, female flies detect the smell and lay their eggs on the meat. Meat and decaying matter is a great place for fly eggs since the maggots that emerge will have lots to eat. When you put the container in a cool, shady place, you allow time for the eggs to hatch and the maggots to appear. With this experiment you are experiencing the fly life cycle first hand!

#4: To the Ant maze!

Note: This experiment requires an **adult's assistance and supervision.**

Materials:

- Two glass jars, one large with lid and one small. The small jar should be able to fit inside of the large jar
- Ants and dirt
- Cotton balls
- Water
- Honey
- Dark colored paper

Procedure:

1. Place the small glass jar upside down inside of the large glass jar. In other words, the bottom of the small glass jar should be facing upwards.

2. **With an adult's help**, locate an ant hill and carefully dig up some of the dirt and capture some of the ants.

3. Ask an adult to make holes in the large glass jar's lid.

4. Transfer the soil and the ants to the large glass jar, filling the space between the two glass jars.

5. Place the lid on the large glass jar and cover the entire jar with brown or dark-colored paper.

6. Soak 3 cotton balls with water, placing a drop of honey on each cotton ball.

7. Put the cotton balls in the large glass jar.

8. Wait a few days and you'll see the ant's begin to tunnel.

What's happening?

Ants are very hard-working bugs. When the paper is wrapped around the jar, it mimic them being underground. Like many animals that live in the soil, ants burrow and make tunnels to travel from the surface of the ground, collecting food, to go back to the ant's nest deep in the soil. The small glass inside of the large glass takes up a lot of space, so the ants are forced to make their tunnels against the walls of the large glass, which makes it really easy for you to see all of their hard-work!

#5: What...bacteria?

Materials:

Bread

Resealable bag

Water

Procedure:

1. Soak the bread in water, until the bread is semi-soaked.
2. Place the bread in the resealable bag and seal.
3. Leave the bread in a warm place for 3-5 days.
4. Observe what starts to grow on the bread.

What's happening?

The bread starts to form mold which is a type of bacteria. Did you know that bacteria were the first organisms on Earth? Scientists have discovered that the first bacteria came from microorganisms that were made by the combination of dirt, gases in the air, and lightning. If is from bacteria that over millions of years, animals and plants slowly evolved.

Quiz

Living things _____ and _____ over time.

1.) Name the three phases of life for animals.
2.) When does most of the growing happen? During what phase of life?
3.) True or False. Death is a natural part of life.
4.) Name two animals that may hatch from an egg.
5.) What happens during the adult phase of life?
6.) Define the phrase *life span*.
7.) Name an animal with a short life span.
8.) Name an animal with a long life span.
9.) Name an animal with a short pregnancy period.
10.) Name an animal with a long pregnancy period.
11.) True or False. Amphibians go through metamorphosis.
12.) Name the stages of the butterfly's life cycle.
13.) What is the difference in the life cycle of a butterfly and the life cycle of a grasshopper?
14.) What is the main job of the adult butterfly?
15.) True or False. Adult butterflies eat a lot during this time.
16.) What does the word metamorphosis mean?
17.) What does the female butterfly have to consider when she lays her eggs?
18.) Why does the female butterfly lay hundreds of eggs at a time?
19.) What happens during the before birth phase of life?

Quiz Answers

1.) Living things grow and develop over time.
2.) The three phases of life for animals are: before birth, young, and adult.
3.) The most growing happens in the young phase, this is when the animal begins to develop from being very small at birth to being much larger at the end of this phase.
4.) True. Death is a natural part of life. During the adult phase, animals reproduce to leave more animals even after their death to continue the life cycle.
5.) Birds and reptiles like snakes and crocodiles hatch from eggs.
6.) During the adult phase growing slows down and the adult's main job is to reproduce and raise offspring.
7.) Life span is how long an animal is likely to live. For some animals this is a very short time, for other animals this is a long period of time.
8.) The butterfly has a short life span. They are expected to live about 2-3 weeks.
9.) The tortoise has a long life span. They can live to be over 100 years old.
10.) A cat has a short pregnancy period of about 2 months.
11.) An elephant has a long pregnancy period of almost 2 years.
12.) True. Amphibians, like the frog go through metamorphosis. It may not be a complete metamorphosis like the butterfly who changes their entire physical appearance, but amphibians are said to do a partial metamorphosis.
13.) The stages of the butterfly's life cycle are: egg, larva (caterpillar), pupa (chrysalis), and adult (butterfly).
14.) The life cycle of a butterfly is an example of complete metamorphosis and has 4 stages and the life cycle of a grasshopper is an example of an incomplete metamorphosis and only has 3 stages.
15.) The main job of the adult butterfly is to reproduce and lay eggs.
16.) False. Adult butterflies do not eat at all during this time. They live off of the stored food that the caterpillar ate during the larva stage.
17.) Metamorphosis means "big change".
18.) The female butterfly has to consider where she lays her eggs and how close the location is to a food source. Caterpillars cannot travel long distances and need to have an immediate food supply after they hatch from the egg.
19.) Not all eggs will hatch and not all caterpillars will develop into a butterfly. The adult female butterfly lays hundreds of eggs hoping that at least a few will develop into butterflies to start the life cycle all over again.
20.) During the birth phase of life there is rapid growth of important structures like the heart, the brain, muscles, and bones.

Life Cycle #3: Plant Development

Like animals, plants also have a life cycle and stages of development. Plants begin their lives as a tiny seed or spore and have to find oil to get nutrients and begin to grow their roots, stems, and leaves.

The green algae is considered to be the ancestor of plants. It was from the green algae millions of years ago that all of the plants we have today came from. There are four types of plants: bryophytes, seedless vascular plants, gymnosperms, and angiosperms. Some of these plant groups are very simple, while others are more complex.

Bryophytes – they are also known by their common name, "moss". These plants have to be near water and cannot grow to be very tall. They reproduce by releasing spores into the air. The spores are then carried by either water or wind and eventually fall to the ground and sprout into more moss. These are the simplest of all plants.

Seedless vascular plants – a fern is an example of this type. These are more complex than the mosses but are not the most advanced plants. These plants can grow to be much taller than the moss because they have a vascular system. What is a vascular system? A vascular system is like your blood vessels in your body. It is a network of channels that helps to carry nutrients and water throughout the plant. This allows plants to be able to grow tall and strong. There is a special channel called the phloem that carries sugars and other nutrients from the plant's leaves down throughout the rest of the plant. There is another special channel called the xylem that carries only water. The xylem carries water from the roots of the plant up through the stem to the plant's leaves.

The seedless vascular plants like the ferns were the first plant to have a vascular system. Ferns reproduce using spores, like the mosses do. This is not the best way to reproduce because a lot of the spores dry out or get washed away and never sprout into new plants.

Gymnosperms – this is a fancy word for "cone-bearing" plants like the pine tree. These are much more complex than the other two plant groups. The pine tree has a vascular system like the ferns and is able to grow very, very tall. Gymnosperms were the first plant group to have seeds not spores. The seeds are in a protective covering called the cone. Pine trees drop their cones and hope that animals will pick it up and bury it for the in topsoil, with enough water and sunlight for it to grow into another tree.

Angiosperms – these are the most complex of all the plant groups. Angiosperms are flowering or fruit-bearing plants like the apple tree or like a rose. These plants also have a vascular system to transport nutrients and also use seeds to reproduce. They also have scents or bright colors to attract pollinators like bees and other insects. For a flower, the pollinator, say a bee, would land and get the nectar from the flower. Some of the plant's pollen would rub off onto the bee. When the bee then leaves and lands on another plant, the pollen would brush off and go into the new plant, helping to fertilize the egg to make a new flower plant.

How does a plant grow?

For plants to grow whether from spores or seeds, they have to absorb enough water. This is important because a seed will stay dormant (meaning will not grow) if there is not enough water in the environment. This is a way for the plant to ensure that there are enough nutrients in the area to help it grow and stay healthy. If there is enough water, the seed will absorb water and then begin to germinate or sprout. Some seeds will not sprout unless they are exposed to very high temperatures like in a fire. Amazingly, after a forest fire, there will be new plants that sprout. That is because they were "awaken" or begin to sprout only **after** they have experienced extreme heats. This helps the forest rebuild itself and grow over time.

Now, let's learn about what plants need to survive.

All plants need soil, water, carbon dioxide (a special kind of gas released from humans), and sunlight. Plants are autotrophs; this means that they can automatically make their own food as long as they have all the things they need. Plants need to make a sugar called glucose. They use sunlight, water, and carbon dioxide to make glucose in a process called photosynthesis. If plants do not have enough water or sunlight, they cannot make their own food and then would starve.

Plants are an essential part of the ecosystem. Plants, including trees, produce oxygen when they go through photosynthesis. Oxygen is needed by humans and animals to survive. Plants and animals form an interesting circle, where plants carbon dioxide from humans and animals, and humans and animals need oxygen from plants. This is why it is devastating when trees and plants are destroyed.

What are the parts of the plant?

Plants have leaves, a stem, and roots. The plant leaves are where photosynthesis happens. This is because the plant's leaves are exposed to the most amount of sunlight. There are special structures in the plant leaf that absorb sunlight and allow for photosynthesis to happen. During the day, plants store as much light as they can in their special structures called chloroplasts and can even do photosynthesis at night when it is dark.

If the glucose (or sugar) for the plant is made in the leaves, how does it get to the rest of the plant? Well, the stem is important in transporting nutrients. You can think of the stem as a highway connecting the leaves to the rest of the plant. In the stem is the xylem which carries water and the phloem which carries the sugars and other nutrients from the leaves to other parts of the plant. The stem grows longer and longer over time to make sure that the leaves are getting enough sunlight.

The roots drill deep into the ground to access water. In some plants like grass, the roots are very wide and not very deep. These are called fibrous roots. For plants with these kinds of roots, the water is near the top of the soil, so the plant's roots do not have to go far into the ground to get the water it needs. For other plants, like a carrot, the root has to go very far down into the ground to get to the water. This long type of root is called a taproot. Taproots are very important during times of drought when the amount of water in the soil may be low. These roots can grow further down through the topsoil to get to water that may be trapped beneath the soil.

Do plants move?

Because plants have very strong roots, they are anchored in place. Plants do not move like animals do and cannot leave if the environment does not have enough nutrients. Plants can however respond to the environment by growing or bending in certain ways.

A plant can bend or grow its stem in one direction if there is more sunlight on one side. For example, if there is more sun on the right side of the plant, it can cause the left side of the stem to grow more, allowing the plant to curve and lean more to the right side to reach the sunlight.

Other plants like ivy can grow toward another plant or an object. For some plants, they continue growing until they touch something. This something could be a tree, another plant, a fence, even a building. Ivy grows toward whatever it is touching. This is why you might see ivy wrapped around a tree, on a gate, or on the side of a building. Some plants grow away from objects or other plants. The petals of a flower can close if touched. This is a way for the plant to try to protect itself.

Plants even respond to gravity. In the growing seed, it can determine which direction the roots have to grow based on gravity. The roots always grow in the same direction with gravity (down) and the stem always grows in the opposite direction of gravity (up).

What is the life cycle of a plant?

Some plants have one life cycle that lasts about one year. These are called annuals and have to be replanted each year. Corn and wheat are examples of annual plants. Other plants are biennials, meaning they have their life cycle lasts two years or two growing seasons. Parsley is an example of a biennial. Lastly, there are perennials. These plants have a much longer life cycle and can be planted once and come back each year. Examples of perennials include lavender, petunias, and lilies.

Activities

Try these interesting plant activities and experiments to learn more about plants, their parts, and what they need to grow.

#1 – Ready, Set, Grow!

Materials:

- Styrofoam cups
- Water
- Plant seeds
- Soil
- Sunlight or bright light to mimic sunlight (a plant lamp works great!)

Procedure

1.) Fill the cups about halfway with soil.
2.) Place the plant seeds into the middle of the soil.
3.) Carefully pour enough water to dampen the soil. Not too much!
4.) Put the cups on a window sill or under the plant light.
5.) Water the plant a little every day and take notes of what you see happening. Be patient! Plants have to do a lot of growing underground, so you may not see anything for a few days.

What's happening?

The seed will sprout when it has enough water. Once the seed sprouts, it will need the light to help it to produce its own food through a process called photosynthesis.

#2 – The light! The light!

Materials:

- Soybean plants (they should be about the same size)
- Fertilizer
- Soil (potting soil is fine)
- Water
- Colored filters or colored transparency sheets (clear, red, green, and blue)
- Very large plastic container (at least 18 – 24 inches in length, 8-12 inches deep, and 6 inches wide)

Procedure:

1.) In the large plastic container, evenly place potting soil. The soil should be 5" deep.

2.) Plant 4 of the soybean plants in 5" of moist potting soil.

3.) Read the fertilizer directions and put in the recommended amount of fertilizer.

4.) Place a different colored filter over each soybean plant. They can be draped over the sides of the container or taped in place.

5.) Place the aquarium in a place that will receive a lot of direct sunlight.

6.) Water the plants each day and take notes about what you see happening and how much each is growing.

What's happening?

Because light gives the plants the energy it needs to create its own food (photosynthesis), the color of the light can be very important. This experiment shows the relationship between light and plant growth.

#3 – Milk, Juice, Soda, and Water…Oh My!

Materials:

- Seeds (green bean seeds work the best!)
- 5 small plant pots
- Potting soil
- A measuring cup
- Whole milk
- Apple or orange Juice
- Soda (any kind is fine)
- Sports Drink like Gatorade or Powerade
- Water
- Black permanent marker

Procedure:

1. Label each plant pot using the black permanent marker. They should be labeled as: "Water/Control," "Juice," "Soda," "Juice," and "Sports Drink."
2. Fill each pot with potting soil about halfway up.
3. Plant three seeds in each of the pots.
4. Measure ½ cup of each liquid and pour it in the plant pot labeled with that liquid. For example, water goes in the "Water/Control" pot, milk goes in the "Milk" pot, etc.

5. Place the pots in a warm, sunny place outdoors or on a sunny window sill indoors.
6. Each day water the plants with the liquid they should get and keep track of their growth.

What's happening?

We know that plants need sunlight, nutrient-rich soil, and water to grow. Although it best for the water to be clean and clear, some plants can grow even when the water is polluted or has a high salt content. Understanding what types of fluids that can help plants grow helps scientists learn more how to help plants and people in times of draught.

#4: The Changing Flower

Materials:

- 3 white carnations
- 3 plastic cups
- Food coloring (you'll need red, green, and blue)
- Water
- Scissors or knife

Procedure:

1. In each of the three plastic cups, fill them halfway with cool water.
2. Place 3-5 drops of food coloring in each cup. For example, place 3 drops of red in one cup, 3 drops of blue in one cup, and 3 drops of green in one cup.
3. Cut the very end of the carnation stems (you should only cut off about ¼ inch of the stem).

4. Place one carnation in each cup and leave for 45 minutes.

What's happening?

The plants roots and stems absorb water. The water travels to the plants leaves and petals. With this experiment the colored water was absorbed and the colors appeared in the petals of the carnation as the water traveled up from the roots through the stem to the top of the plant.

#5: Amazing Clay Plant Balls

Materials:

- Clay (modeling clay is best)
- Wax paper
- Potting soil (you can get this from your local hardware or gardening store)
- Plant seeds

Procedure:

1. Soften the clay by kneading it with your hands.
2. Flatten the clay and make it into a small circular disc. This should have a 4-6 inch diameter.
3. Put a small handful of potting soil on top of the clay.
4. Place a few plant seeds on top of the soil.
5. Fold the clay so that the potting soil and seeds are on the inside of the clay.
6. Roll the clay into a ball. The soil and seeds should now be in the inside of the clay ball.
7. Place a handful of soil and the remaining seeds on a flat surface and roll the clay ball over them. They should start to stick on the outside of the clay ball.

8. Set the clay ball on the wax paper and leave for 2 days, or until the clay has dried out.

9. Plant the clay ball in your backyard and watch the plants grow!

What's happening?

Some environments are very dry and this makes it very hard for seeds to sprout and grow. By having the soil and seeds mixed with clay allows the moisture and water to stay and keep the seeds healthy. The soil inside of the seed ball is a food source for the growing seeds inside of the ball. The seeds will be protected inside of the clay until there is enough rainwater to wash the clay away and allow the seed to sprout and grow into a plant.

Quiz

Check Your Understanding

1.) What are the three plant groups?
2.) What plant group does not have a vascular system?
3.) What is a vascular system?
4.) True or False. The xylem carries water throughout the plant.
5.) True or False. The phloem carries nutrients and sugars up from the roots to the leaves.
6.) Which is the most complex plant group?
7.) What is a seed?
8.) Name the three parts of the plant.
9.) _____ is like the plant's highway to transport nutrients.
10.) Give an example of a plant that grows toward touch.
11.) _____ _____ is the ancestor of all plants.
12.) What will happen if one side of the plant is exposed to more light than the other side?
13.) Plants are autotrophs which mean they _____ _____ _____ _____.
14.) True or false. Plants go through photosynthesis to make their own food.
15.) Name at least 3 things plants need to survive.
16.) The _____ grow in the same direction as gravity.
17.) The _____ grows in the opposite direction as gravity.
18.) What is the difference between a fibrous root and a taproot?
19.) How long is the life cycle of a biannual?
20.) True or false. A perennial has to be replanted each year.

Quiz Answers

1.) The three plant groups are the bryophytes (moss), the seedless vascular plants (ferns), the gymnosperms (cone-bearing plants), and the angiosperms (fruit-bearing plants).
2.) The bryophytes or mosses do not have a vascular system. Since they cannot transport nutrients throughout the plant, they do not grow very tall.
3.) It is a way for plants to transport nutrients and water throughout the plant. The vascular system is made up of the xylem and the phloem.
4.) True. The xylem carries water throughout the plant.
5.) False. The phloem carries nutrients and sugars, but it carries it down from the leaves through the rest of the plant to the roots. The xylem runs in the opposite direction, carrying water up from the roots to the plant's leaves.
6.) The angiosperms or flowering/fruit-bearing plants are the most complex plant group.
7.) A seed is a protective covering where the growing plant lives until it sprouts to form a new plant.
8.) The roots, stem, and leaves are the three parts of the plant.
9.) The stem is like the plant's highway to transport nutrients. It is inside of the stem where the xylem and phloem are.
10.) An ivy or a vine is an example of a plant that grows toward other objects or toward whatever it is touching.
11.) The green algae is the ancestor of all plants.
12.) The plant will make its stem longer on the side opposite the light so that the stem can bend toward the light.
13.) Plants are autotrophs which mean they make their own food.
14.) True. Plants go through photosynthesis to make their own food. This happens in the leaves where they are exposed to sunlight.
15.) Plants need water, soil, carbon dioxide, and sunlight to survive.
16.) The roots grow in the same direction as gravity.
17.) The stem grows in the opposite direction as gravity.
18.) A fibrous root is wide, not deep. This is for plants that do not need to drill down deep in the soil for water. However, a taproot is long and is needed for plants that have to go deep into the soil to access water.
19.) The life cycle of a biannual last two growing seasons or two years.
20.) False. A perennial does not have to be replanted each year. An annual plant like corn or wheat has to be planted each year. Perennials are able to live for more than two growing seasons and may need to be replanted every 3-5 years.

Earth Science #1: Rocks

Did you know that there are different types of rocks? In fact, there are three different types of rocks: sedimentary, metamorphic, and igneous. We will go through each type of rock in this section. It is important to remember that rocks can start of as one type of rock, but over the course of thousands of years, can change into another type of rock. We will discuss this rock phenomenon throughout this section.

Sedimentary Rock

Sand, broken shells, and smaller rocks or pebbles form what is called sediment. Over time, the sediment builds up in layers and then starts to harden to form rock. Since the sediment are different types of materials with different size particles and textures, sedimentary rock is relatively soft and is very brittle. This is the type of rock where fossils can be found. We'll talk a lot more about fossils in a later section. Limestone is an example of sedimentary rock.

Sedimentary rock gives rise to coal and petroleum. Over three-quarters of the Earth's surface is covered in sedimentary rock.

Metamorphic Rock

In science the term metamorphosis means to undergo a change. Metamorphic rock is formed within Earth and is made by exerting extreme pressure and heat. These types of rocks appear to be shiny and are made very slowly. Marble is an example of metamorphic rock.

Igneous Rock

Deep within the layers of the Earth is a layer called the mantle. The mantle contains magma which is a super-hot liquid substance. Magma can come to the Earth's surface, like during the eruption of a volcano, and cool to form rock. Magma can also cool without coming to the Earth's surface. When magma hardens in the crust, it forms a type of igneous rock called granite. Granite takes a long time to cool, but when it does, it is very hard and not easily broken. Most mountains are made of this type of igneous rock.

This type of rock is characterized by looking like glass and often has pockets of gas trapped inside the solid structure. These gas pockets leave tiny holes in the cooled rock. Basalt or volcanic rock is an example of igneous rock.

Mountains are an interesting phenomenon as it relates to rock and rock formation. New mountains are often tall and have jagged edges along its surface. Over millions of years, new mountains turn into old mountains, which are more rounded and shorter in height. Why do mountains shrink? The rock on the mountain gets worn down through a process called rock erosion. We'll talk more about rock erosion later in this section. The bits of rock that are lost or chipped off from the mountain form the sediment that then can be combined to create sedimentary rock. So, igneous rock from mountains, can then be made into sedimentary rock millions of years later.

The layers of Earth are made of rocks. The outermost layer, the crust, has a top layer made of soil, sand, broken rocks, and water. Digging deeper into the crust, you will find rocks of all types. Right below the soil layer (where we plant and dig) is a solid layer of rock called bedrock.

What is the rock cycle?

Rocks have a life cycle, just like animals do. They are formed, worn down, broken, and reformed all the time. The rock cycle is hundreds, if not thousands of years long. There are six steps of the rock cycle. We will go through each.

Step 1: Weathering and Erosion

What is weathering? Weathering can either be a physical process or a chemical process. During physical weathering pieces of rock are broken down to form sediment. Chemical weather, on the other hand, involves the dissolving of minerals within the rock, changing the composition of the rock altogether.

What is erosion? Think of it this way…everything in nature wears down over time. Just like our bodies and muscles may wear down as we age, so too do rocks. Erosion is a necessary part of the rock cycle as this is what provides sediment to then form sedimentary rock. Rock erosion can be dangerous, especially if large boulders chip off of a mountain's surface or if the rock that supports a house wears down. The good thing is rock erosion takes a long time to occur, as the rock is exposed to rain, hot and cold temperatures, and wind.

Step 2: Rock Transport

Once erosion has occurred, rock particles (sediment) may be moved by wind, animals, or some form of water like rain, streams or oceans. These rock particles begin to accumulate near one another and begin to set the stage for new rock formation.

Step 3: Deposition

The sediment is able to travel, in some cases, very far distances, until they settle and begin to collect. Sediment then starts to mix with soil and forms a new layer of sediment. Over time, these groups of floating layers of sediment can create rock islands.

Step 4: Compaction and Cementation

Layers of sediment can stack on top of one another, causing pressure to build up one the lower layers. This pressure can force the sediment particles to come so close together that they are able to form new solids. The spaces in between neighboring sediment particles are often filled with dissolved minerals, like calcium to make the new rock. Since this rock is made by compacting sediment together, this is how sedimentary rock is formed.

Step 5: Metamorphism

Sedimentary rock can be formed deep within the Earth's layers under thousands of tons of other rocks. The more these rocks get forced deeper into the ground the more pressure put upon them and the higher the temperature is around them. This extreme pressure and heat can change the shape of these rocks from being sedimentary to metamorphic rock. Eventually these rocks get pushed so deep into the Earth's crust that they go into the hot mantle or magma and are melted.

Step 6: Rock Melting

Rocks can actually melt! This is true when metamorphic rocks are pushed into the magma. When rocks melt, they become part of the super-hot magma, which can then go to the Earth's surface and cool to make igneous rock. This starts the rock cycle all over again!

Special Types of Rock Formations

Have you ever been inside of a cavern? In caverns there are special rock formations made from minerals like calcium. There are some rock formations that emerge from the ceiling and grow down toward the ground. These are called stalactites. Other rock formations emerge from the ground and grow tall toward the ceiling. These are called stalagmites. There is an easy way to remember which rock formation is which by looking at the names of each. Stala**c**tites have a "c" in their name, which will help you remember that they are on the **c**eiling. Whereas stalagmites have a "g" since they start on the **g**round. These types of rock formations can also be called dripstones because they are made from water moving calcium deposits. As the water "drips" from the tips of these rock formations, it adds more calcite (a special form of calcium) to the growing formation. This process takes thousands of years to happen!

What about precious stones?

Some rocks are considered to be precious stones or gems. These are rare crystals made of minerals. Depending on the type of mineral, the gem may look different and have different shapes. For example, diamond is made of a collection of carbon, whereas rubies are made by the mineral corundum.

Some precious stones are very hard and not easily broken. Diamond is the hardest of the gems. Other precious stones are very brittle such as emeralds. Precious stones have to be harvested or dug up from the ground. In some cases, people may dig with shovels and screen or sort through the soil to find precious stones. In other instances, people may do cave mining and travel into caves, breaking the walls to find precious stones that may lie beneath the rock's surface. The rarity and the quality of the precious stone helps to determine its value. Very rare stones like Tanzanite, a blue-purple colored stone are found only near Mount Kilimanjaro, in Northern Tanzania. This makes it very rare and very valuable, especially to jewelers.

The Hope Diamond is the most famous precious stone in the world. It is not your average diamond. Instead, the Hope Diamond is blue-white in color. It is so rare that it is kept in a museum in Washington, D.C.

As you have learned in this section, rocks can come in a wide variety of shapes, sizes, and colors. Rocks are not as boring as they may appear because rocks are always changing and going through the rock cycle. Starting a rock collection is a fun and easy way to study rocks like geologists do! Rocks hold a wealth of information about the past and about the composition of Earth. We can find fossils in some types of rocks and even learn about past animal and plant life. Next time you pick up a rock, think about where it came from and what it may become thousands of years from now.

Activities

Try these cool rock experiments to test your understanding of rocks, the types, and the rock cycle.

#1- Chart that rock!

Materials:

- Poster board or large sheet of white paper
- Black marker or pen
- Sticky notes

Procedure:

1. In the center of the poster board, draw a large circle. Around the circle draw 5 straight lines coming from the circle.
2. Draw multiple lines coming from the circle.
3. Using the sticky notes, write one fact you learned about rocks and place it at the end of each line. If you can think of more than 5 facts about rocks, draw more lines and keep going!

What's happening?

When you learn a new concept, it is important to reflect on what you learned and write it down. This activity should get you thinking about what you do know and what you have learned about rocks. Keep this in your room as a reminder of all the cool and interesting things you know about rocks!

#2 – Sand, Pebbles, and Glue—Oh My!

Materials:

- Sand
- Small rocks or pebbles
- Liquid glue
- Large clear plastic cup

Procedure:

1) Place a thin layer of sand in the bottom of the cup.

2) Pour the liquid glue into the cup and then add several of the small rocks. Be careful not to add too much glue, though, because the rocks will take longer to dry.

3) Repeat steps 1-2 until the cup is about 2 inches full.

4) Place the cups in a window sill (with lots of sunlight) for the cups to dry.

5) After a week, the materials should be dry.

6) With an adult's help, cut the cup away and, voila, you have your very own rock!

What's happening?

The sand, small rocks, and glue bond together to form a solid object, much like the rock you might see in the backyard.

#3 - Why kick rocks when you can eat them?!

Note: This experiment requires **adult assistance and supervision**.

Materials

- Aluminum foil
- Wax paper
- Starburst candy
- Toaster oven
- Towels
- Flat surface

Procedure

1.) Unwrap the Starburst candy.

2.) Lay the aluminum foil flat on the table and place the square of wax paper on top.

3.) Stack the 3 different Starburst in the middle of the squares

4.) Wrap the papers around the Starburst tightly, making sure to mold the foil around the shape of the Starburst.

5.) Because sedimentary rocks are made by pressure over time to "make" a sedimentary rock formation apply pressure. This can be done by squishing the Starburst with your hands or pressing it down against the table.

6.) Metamorphic rocks are made by heat and pressure. To make metamorphic rocks ask an adult's help to wrap the Starburst in foil and place it in the toaster oven for approximately 2 minutes or until the Starburst is soft but not melting. Then, wrap the "rock" in a towel and apply pressure. After the "rocks" have cooled and been pressed, remove the foil and wax paper to see your new metamorphic rock!

7.) Igneous rock is created from extreme heat. To make igneous rocks, the Starburst (wrapped in wax paper and foil) should be placed in the toaster oven on high heat for about 5-10 minutes. The Starburst should be melting but not burnt when it comes out of the oven. Once it is melted, ask an adult to carefully open the foil and wax paper and take a quick peek. Let the candy cool.

What's happening?

You are able to see how the three different types of rock are formed from start to finish. Seeing the different "rock" pattern by using candy is a great and yummy way to better understand what each rock type looks like and why they look that way.

#4: Deep Freeze!

Materials:

- Rocks, like limestone, granite, and sandstone (these can be found at your local hardware or gardening store)
- Empty plastic water bottle
- Water

Procedure:

1. Examine the rock. Take a note of its size and shape.
2. Place the rock in the water bottle.
3. Fill the bottle with water and place the lid on it.
4. Put the water bottle in the freezer for 6 hours.
5. Take the water bottle out and let it thaw out.
6. Repeat steps 3 and 4 at least three more times.

7. Carefully take the rock out and look at it. What has changed?

What's happening?

Remember that rocks get broken down or erode over time by being exposed to the wind, the rain, and by hitting other rocks. Rocks are also weathered by being frozen and then thawing. When a rock freezes, the water seeps into the small cracks in the rock and as the water turns into ice, it expands. This causes even bigger cracks in the rock. When the rock thaws and the ice melts, the rock has larger spaces than it did before. The process keeps continuing until pieces of the rock completely break off.

#5: The Absorbent Rock

Materials:

- Chalk
- Water
- Cup

Procedure:

1. Place one piece of chalk in the cup.
2. Fill the cup with water.
3. Let sit for 24 hours.
4. Carefully pour out the water. What do you notice about the chalk?

What's happening?

Rocks are solid, but they do have small cracks or openings in them. These openings can allow rocks to absorb water. These are called porous rocks and chalk is one of these types of rocks. Chalk is made up of calcium carbonate, similar to an egg's shell. The chalk is able to absorb water, it takes time, but it is a type of natural rock sponge.

Quiz

Check Your Understanding

1.) Name the three different types of rocks
2.) What type of rock is formed under extreme heat and pressure?
3.) Sand, broken shells and smaller pebbles make _____.
4.) What is an example of igneous rock?
5.) _____ is a super-hot liquid substance in the Earth's mantle.
6.) Mountains are which type of rock?
7.) What is the difference between a new mountain and an old mountain?
8.) What is below the soil layer?
9.) Rocks are formed, worn down, and reformed during the _____.
10.) What is rock erosion?
11.) How are rock pieces transported?
12.) What is weathering?
13.) Name the six steps of the rock cycle?
14.) What occurs during the cementation step of the rock cycle?
15.) True or False. Rocks can undergo melting.
16.) Name the rock structure that is attached to the ground of a cavern and grows to the ceiling.
17.) Name the rock structure that is attached to the ceiling of a cavern and grows to the ground.
18.) Diamond is made of _____.
19.) Name three types of precious stones.
20.) What is the most famous precious stone?

Quiz Answers

1.) The three types of rock are: sedimentary, metamorphic, and igneous.
2.) Metamorphic rocks are formed under extreme heat and pressure. This often occurs in the mantle of the Earth which is a super-hot liquid type substance.
3.) Sand, broken shells and smaller pebbles make sediment.
4.) Granite is an example of an igneous rock.
5.) Magma is a super-hot liquid substance in the Earth's mantle.
6.) Mountains are a type of igneous rock. They are formed when magma reaches the Earth's surface and is cooled.
7.) New mountains are tall and have jagged sides. Old mountains because of rock erosion over time are shorter and more round/smooth.
8.) Bedrock is below the soil layer. This is a solid layer of rock.
9.) Rocks are formed, worn down, and reformed during the rock cycle.
10.) Rock erosion is when rocks are worn down over time. This can happen because they are exposed to rain and wind and can also happen when rocks are under extreme pressure.
11.) Rock pieces that break off during rock erosion are often transported by the wind and water.
12.) Weathering is the natural breakdown of rock. This can be due to physical or chemical processes.
13.) The six steps of the rock cycle are: weathering and erosion, rock transport, deposition, compaction and cementation, metamorphosis, and rock melting.
14.) The rock pieces or sediment is forced together and begins to form one large piece of rock.
15.) True, rocks can melt. This is one of the steps of the rock cycle and this occurs when the rock is pushed into the hot magma in the Earth's mantle.
16.) Stalagmites are attached to the ground of a cavern and grow toward the ceiling.
17.) Stalactites are attached to the ceiling of a cavern and grow toward the ground.
18.) Diamond is made of carbon.
19.) Three precious stones are: diamonds, rubies, and emeralds.
20.) The Hope Diamond is the most famous precious stone. It is owned by the Smithsonian museum in Washington, D.C.

Earth Science #2: Soil

You just learned about rocks and when they break down to smaller pieces called sediment. Sediment is an essential part of what forms soil or dirt. When rocks continue to break down into smaller and smaller pieces, this forms sand. Sand particles are very tiny.

Plants can sprout in sandy areas and as plants die and are broken down by bacteria, these "stuff" mixes with the sand to form soil. Soil is necessary for life on Earth. Plants could not live without having soil and water for their roots. Likewise, there are a lot of animals that could not live without plants, and this would trickle all the way up to humans.

What are the many names of soil?

You may call soil, "dirt". Soil can also be called clay, silt, or humus. Wet soil forms mud. Soil is located on the outermost part of the Earth, along the crust. There are many layers of soil, with some layers being more nutrient rich for the plants to get nutrients and other layers may be nutrient poor.

Have you ever heard of topsoil? Topsoil is the layer of soil that has the most nutrients for plants to use. Gardeners often buy topsoil from hardware stores and use it in their gardens to help give their plants the nutrients they need to grow and be healthy. Soil is made up of varying amounts of minerals and living and dead matter.

What's living matter?

The soil is the home to plant roots, small insects like caterpillars or ants. These are considered living matter as they are alive and grow. Many organisms call the soil home because it is often damp, cool, and a great place to burrow or hide from predators.

What's dead matter?

Death is a part of the natural life cycle of animals and plants. When a leaf falls from a tree, it will land on the surface of the soil and over time, it will break apart and decompose. The nutrients that were in the leaf will now get absorbed by the soil and these nutrients can then be reabsorbed or used by other plants in the soil. When an animal dies, the same process occurs. The animal's body decomposes and releases important nutrients into the soil for other organisms to use to grow.

Fungi like mushrooms and bacteria are important in helping to break down dead matter to recycle their nutrients. Bacteria are also important in taking nutrients from the air such as nitrogen and converting it into a form that can be absorbed in the soil. This is similar to what fertilizers do. Fertilizers provide soil with important nutrients like nitrogen if there is not enough in the soil already.

How is soil made?

Plant roots are an important part of making soil. As plants' roots grow deeper into the soil, sometimes breaking through rock, more soil is made. Roots also cause the soil to be loose and not compacted together. This benefits insects and animals living in the soil as it allows them spaces to move and travel in the soil, but it also allows for oxygen to enter the soil. Oxygen is an important gas that animals (and humans) need to survive. If the soil was too tightly packed, it would squeeze out all of the oxygen, making it impossible for animals and insects to breath.

What nutrients are needed in the soil?

Plants rely on the soil to give them the nutrients they need to grow. What do you think would happen if the soil does not have any more nutrients for plants? The plants would eventually die. Plants are sessile, meaning they cannot move. So, if there are no nutrients (or not enough) for them in their current location, they cannot get up and move like animals can. In order for plants to be healthy, they need:

Nitrogen – This is an important nutrient found in fertilizers and this helps leaves and stems to grow. Leaves are the structures the plant uses to make its own food. Without them, the plant would starve. The stem helps the plant to grow toward the Sun. The Sun and light are essential to a plant's development. In order to make its own food, a plant needs the sunlight to start the process. This is similar to you needing a fire on the stove to cook pasta. Without the fire, the pasta wouldn't cook.

Phosphate – This nutrient helps fruits and roots to develop. Roots are needed to help the plant dig deep into the soil to find water. Water is such an important substance in all animal and plant life.

Potassium – This helps to maintain plant health. Plants do not need large amounts of potassium, but without even small amounts, plants could die. Some plants like bananas store potassium in large amounts and bananas are a great source of potassium for humans and animals!

What are the layers of soil?

Soil forms layers also called horizons. There are three soil horizons: topsoil, subsoil, and bedrock.

Topsoil – This is the upper layer of soil. When you touch the ground, you are touching the top soil layer. This is the layer where plants get nutrients like nitrogen, phosphate and potassium to grow. This layer of soil is easy to spot. It is often a very dark brown color and may contain dead and decaying matter such as leaves, dead plants, etc. In order for the topsoil to remain rich in nutrients dead matter must be added and decayed. Remember soil itself is not alive, so it cannot make nutrients on its own. Instead, the plants depend on other things like fallen plants and leaves and dead animals to decompose and recycle their nutrients into the topsoil.

Subsoil – if you dig deeper, past the topsoil layer, you will hit the subsoil. This layer looks more like clay and is important for storing water for plants. A plant's roots will begin in the topsoil layer, but grow deep into the ground into the subsoil to get to the water. The subsoil can be moved or washed away very easily through erosion, so it is important that it stays covered by the topsoil layer.

Bedrock – This is the lowest layer of soil. You would have to dig at least 3 miles into the ground to hit bedrock. In some places, you may have to dig even further down past the top two layers of soil to get to this layer. Bedrock can also be called the parent layer because this layer as it breaks down and moves upward forms the subsoil and also the topsoil layers.

Knowing the different soil layers is part of the battle. Soil can be classified based on the types of particles within it. Take for example clay soils. This type of soil has a lot of small particles and not a lot of nutrients, making this the least suitable type of soil for plant growth. In addition, clay soils are so tightly packed that there is no room for oxygen to be stored in the soil and there is little to no water. Sandy soils have a lot of large particles. This leaves very large spaces in the soil for oxygen or water to be stored. In comparison to clay soil, sandy soil can be good for plant growth since there is water and oxygen present within the soil.

What is soil erosion?

You learned about rock erosion earlier. The same process can happen to the soil. When it rains, the topsoil can be carried by the rain water and collect in other places like in streams, rivers, and oceans. When the soil moves, it may take key nutrients with it. Think about what would happen if your house was built on a hill. Over time, the soil from the hill may be washed away and your house could be in danger of sliding off of the hill. This phenomenon is often referred to as a "landslide" or a "mudslide". When nutrients levels in the soil are low, rainfall can leave the remaining soil without any nutrients for the plants to use. This is what occurs in the tropical rainforest. The tropical rainforest is home to thousands of exotic plants and animals, but also has the worse soil. This is because of the high amount of rainfall. Every year, the tropical rainforest has almost one foot (12 inches) of rainfall. That's a lot of rain! With every rainfall, more and more of the nutrients in the topsoil are washed away.

Here are some interesting soil facts:

1.) Soil has been an influential part of everyday life for millions of years. It has been used to make food, clothing, medicines, even paper! In some ancient civilizations, mud from the soil was used to build homes.

2.) Each year millions of tons of soil is eroded or washed away.

3.) Farmers can help to keep soil healthy and full of nutrients by rotating crops. This means that one year a farmer may plant corn, but the next year he/she may plant wheat. Because plants are different, different crops will use different amounts of nutrients. By changing the crop every year or every two years, farmers can make sure that the levels of important nutrients stay high.

Activities

#1 – Soil, Soil Everywhere

Materials:

- Clay soil
- Soil loam
- Sandy soil
- Plastic cups or jars
- Coffee filters
- Rubber bands

Procedure

1. Set out three cups or jars.
2. Attach coffee filters to tops of the cups or jars using rubber bands.
3. Place the different soils on different jars. For example, one for clay soil, one for sandy soil, and one for soil loam).
4. Pour water over each of the soils to see what happens to the water as it passes through each type of soil.

What's happening?

The water is absorbed better by the soil loam, which means that it is a better soil for planting.

#2 Yummy Soil!

Materials

- Clear plastic cups (larger cups are better for this project)
- Paper plates
- Marshmallows (small to medium size)

- Cheerios
- Chocolate rice crispies
- Mini M&Ms
- Gummy worms

Procedure

1. Put marshmallows in the very bottom of the cup because it will represent the bedrock.
2. Cheerios should be the next layer, representing the subsoil. You can put in whole Cheerios or mash them up.
3. Above the Cheerios will be the chocolate rice crispies with mini M&Ms mixed in. The rice crispies represent the topsoil and the M&Ms represent humus.
4. To finish, add in a couple gummy worms.

What's happening?

Looking at all of the layers of soil can be difficult because the layers can be hundreds of feet deep. Using these ingredients help us see what the layers look like, without having to dig hundreds of feet into the ground. Plus, it is tastier this way!

#3: Soil Mix-Up

Materials:

- Soil (this should be from your backyard)
- Two large glass jars with lids
- Spoon

Procedure:

1. Fill one glass jar one-third of the way full with soil.
2. Fill one glass jar with clean water.
3. Add the water from the jar in step 2 to the jar from step 1, until the soil and water jar is almost full.

4. Use the spoon to mix the soil and water mixture.

5. Leave the jar for one hour. What do you see? Can you see the contents of the jar? Are there different layers?

What's happening?

When the jar is left undisturbed the contents in the soil starts to separate. The bottom layer is where the sand is since it has the largest sized particles. Silt will be on top of the sand layer. If there was clay in the soil, then that would be on the top layer. The water at the very top will not be clear because it will have decaying plant material also called organic material.

#4: No Dirt Needed!

Materials:

- Sweet potato
- Glass cup
- Water
- Toothpicks

Procedure:

1. Put three toothpicks into the sweet potato, in the large end. The toothpicks should stick out in all directions.

2. Take the glass cup and fill it more than half way with water.

3. Put the sweet potato into the water with the end with the toothpicks sticking up and resting on the opening of the glass jar. The toothpicks should be holding the sweet potato upside down into the glass.

4. Place the glass cup in a sunny place and leave for at least 3 days.

5. Watch the vine grow from the sweet potato without using water!

What's happening?

Some plants, like the sweet potato can grow without nutrients from the soil. The sweet potato is able to live off of the sugars it made during photosynthesis. These sugars give the plant the energy it needs to sprout into a plant.

#5: Who's There?

Materials:

- Soil (this works best with soil from your yard)
- Glass jar with lid
- Lime water (this can be purchased at a grocery store)
- Small dixie cup (this needs to be able to fit inside of the glass jar

Procedure:

1. Place a few handfuls of soil into the glass jar.
2. Fill the cup with lime water.
3. Place the dixie cup into the jar, resting it on top of the soil.
4. Seal the glass jar with the lid and let the jar sit untouched for 2 days. What do you see?

What's happening?

The lime water changed from being a yellowish clear liquid to milky white. Why is that? There are small organisms that live in the soil. Most you can't see with your eyes, you'd have to use a microscopic. These organisms breathe in oxygen and release carbon dioxide. The carbon dioxide mixed with the lime water to turn it to a milky white color.

Quiz

1.) How is soil formed?
2.) True or False. Sand particles are very large.
3.) What are two other names for soil?
4.) What are the layers of soil?
5.) Which layer of soil has the most nutrients for plants?
6.) True or False. The subsoil layer stores water.
7.) Give an example of living matter.
8.) _____ help to break down dead animals and plants to give nutrients to the soil.
9.) A plant's roots can break through _____ to form more soil.
10.) _____ is important because it helps the leaves of a plant form and develop?
11.) True or False. Without phosphate the fruit on a fruit tree would not grow.
12.) What layer of soil is made up of clay?
13.) If you dug 3 miles down into the ground, you would hit the _____ layer.
14.) Name the layer of soil that erodes or gets washed away very quickly.
15.) A mudslide can occur when what happens?
16.) Name three things that we get from the soil.
17.) True or False. The tropical rainforest has the most nutrients in its topsoil.
18.) Framers can keep the topsoil healthy by _____ _____.
19.) What causes soil erosion?
20.) What organism needs soil the most?

Quiz Answers

1.) Soil is formed when bits of rocks and decomposing matter are broken down.
2.) False. Sand particles are very tiny.
3.) Soil can also be called dirt, humus, clay or silt.
4.) There are three layers, they are: topsoil, subsoil, and bedrock.
5.) The top layer or the topsoil has the most nutrients for plants. This is where nutrients from dead leaves and animals are absorbed.
6.) True. The subsoil layer stores water.
7.) Answers may vary. Living matter is anything that is alive. This can include plants, insects, and animals.
8.) Bacteria help to break down dead animals and plants to give nutrients to the soil. Fungi are also important with breaking down dead matter as well.
9.) A plant's roots can break through rock to form more soil. This is what actually helps to form new soil.
10.) Nitrogen is important because it helps the leaves of a plant form and develop? Nitrogen is often in fertilizers for this very reason.
11.) True. Without phosphate the fruit on a fruit tree would not grow. Phosphate helps with fruit develop and the growth of the plant's roots.
12.) The subsoil is made up of clay. This allows it to store water. A plant's roots will begin in the topsoil, but will need to grow into the subsoil to get access to stored water.
13.) If you dug 3 miles down into the ground, you would hit the bedrock layer. This is the layer that is solid rock. It is often called the parent layer because as the rock within the bedrock layer erodes, they are pushed upward to form new soil.
14.) The subsoil erodes or gets washed away very quickly. To prevent this it has to be covered by the topsoil.
15.) A mudslide can occur when the soil erodes or is washed away over time. This is very dangerous and can lead to homes being damaged.
16.) From the soil we can get things to make medicines, clothing, and use soil for buildings.
17.) False. The tropical rainforest's topsoil is low in nutrients. This is because of the high rainfall. With each rain more and more of the topsoil and its nutrients gets washed away.
18.) Framers can keep the topsoil healthy by rotating crops. Rotating crops helps to keep the nutrient levels high since different crops use different amounts of nutrients to grow and develop.
19.) Exposure to the wind or rainfall causes soil erosion.
20.) Plants need the soil the most. However, animals (including humans) depend on plants for lots of things. Without soil, there would be no plant life, but without plants, there would also be no animal life. All organisms are interconnected in this way.

Earth Science #3: Environmental or Natural Resources

Let's start to put all the pieces of what you have learned together. There are lots of things we get from the environment, we'll review them now.

Rocks – You learned that rocks help to form the soil for plants. Rocks are also important in providing shelter for animals. Think about all the animals that may live on the side of a mountain or inside of a cave. Rocks also store minerals like calcium and phosphorus which are needed by plants and animals to grow and develop.

Earlier, we talked about precious stones. What do you think they are used for? Precious stones like diamonds, rubies, emeralds, and even opal are used for jewelry. This has been a practice for thousands of years. Even the Ancient Egyptians used precious stones for jewelry and to signify royalty and wealth.

Rocks have been used to make weapons or tools. Native Americans would use obsidian, a type of igneous rock to make arrow heads for hunting or for war weapons. The early cavemen would sharpen stones to make simple tools to hit or cut other objects.

Today, we use rocks for buildings, to make strong foundations. Rocks can also be used for decorative purposes like in a garden or for a backyard patio or walkway. Sculptors often use stone to carve figures out of or make statues. Take for example, Mount Rushmore. This is an elaborate stone carving on the side of a mountain with the faces of four famous presidents. The neat thing about stone or rock carvings is that they can last for hundreds of years before they erode. This wouldn't be true with paper or a painting, which would easily get damaged during a rainstorm or in the intense summer heat.

Water – Is the most important substance on Earth. Without water, life would not exist. So what exactly does what help with? Water is an essential part of:

- Temperature regulation: What happens if you are very hot? You sweat! Your body has pores in your skin to release water to help cool you off. Because water is such a strong substance, when it evaporates (goes from liquid to gas), it takes a lot of your body heat with it, leaving you feeling cooler. Did you know water helps to regulate the temperature of the ocean? Yes, it does! In the winter, ice freezes and floats to the ocean's surface. This layer of ice helps to block some of the cold air from getting into the ocean. This leaves the ocean water slightly warmer than the ocean's surface. This does not mean that it is very hot, but is slightly warmer, warm enough for fish, whales, penguins, and other aquatic animals to live through the harsh winter. When the Spring emerges and the temperatures increase, the layer of ice is the first to melt. As the heats up and melts, the liquid water from the melting goes down into the ocean and the ocean water rotates, bringing nutrients from the ocean's surface to the bottom of the ocean.

- Nutrient Transport: Water is what we call the universal solvent. What does that mean? It means that water can dissolve most things. Water cannot dissolve everything, but it can does a lot of important things that our bodies need dissolved. Think about it this way…if water could not dissolve other substances, then we would be unable to move nutrients around our bodies in our bloodstream. Water also helps plants move nutrients throughout the plant's stem and leaves.

- Chemical Reactions: Water is a necessary substance in important chemical reactions that take place in nature. Without water the reactions would not take place at all or be very slow. For example, plants need water to make their own food. The energy from water is combined with the energy from the sunlight to help plants make a special sugar called glucose. This glucose is what the plants needs and uses to survive.

Plants – Plants help other organisms stay healthy. Plants make their own food with sunlight, water, and carbon dioxide (a special gas in the air). Plants are one of the only organisms that can do this. Other organisms like animals have to eat other organisms to get energy. Let's look at the food chain (on the right) to better understand the importance of plants in the ecosystem.

A food chain shows how animals are eaten. The arrow indicates who eats what animal. For example the frog is eaten by the snake and the insect is eaten by the frog. The plant is at the bottom of the food chain. This means that without plants, there would be nothing for the insect to eat. What do you think would eventually happen? The insect would either move to another habitat or die out from starvation. But, then how would that affect the frog? The frog would not have anything to eat if there are not enough insects. So, the frogs may die out. But, then what would happen to the snakes? The snakes would die out and then the eagle would have no food to eat. As you can see, the plant is the foundation or holds up the food chain. Without plants, the other animals would suffer and could die.

We often say that plants are the primary producers. This means that they are the first food source in an ecosystem. We get lots of food from plants like corn, wheat, fruits, nuts, even maple syrup.

Plants are also important in textiles or clothing, building, and in medicine.

If you think of bamboo or an oak tree, they can be used to build homes and they were, and still are, an important building source for hundreds of years. Where do you think rubber comes from? It actually comes from a tree! The rubber tree produces rubber that we use to make plastics of all sorts.

We get cotton from the cotton plant. The cotton can then be woven to make fabrics and the fabrics can be used for various items inside and outside of the home.

Did you know that many plants are herbs that can be used as natural ways to cure illness? The daffodil is used to treat Alzheimer's and the Foxglove plant has been used since the 1500s to treat heart disease.

Not only do plants provide us with food and materials, but they also serve as homes or habitats for thousands of animals. Squirrels, birds, even some snakes live in trees and rely on the tree for shade and shelter from predators.

Where does the oxygen we breathe come from? This comes from plants and trees also! When plants make their own food through a process called photosynthesis, they release oxygen. This is the only way that oxygen is made. If we were to cut down all of the trees and plants, then no more oxygen would be made and animals and humans would be unable to survive. Aquatic plants like seaweed also release oxygen into the oceans for animals like fish and dolphins to breathe. As plants make their own food they use up carbon dioxide. Carbon dioxide is a gas that we release when we breathe out or exhale. It is also released by factories and cars. The only way it can be removed is through photosynthesis. Reducing the levels of carbon dioxide in the air is a good thing for the environment. This helps to reduce the greenhouse effect which is causing the Earth to warm quicker than it should. Plants and animals need each other. Plants need carbon dioxide from animals and animals need the oxygen that the plants make.

Soil – Why is dirt important? Well, dirt or soil as you learned contains nutrients that plants need to grow. Without soil, plants would die out and we discussed the consequences that could have on other animals. Soil can also be a great storage system not just for nutrients but also for water.

Soil also supports life, literally. If we didn't have dirt, we would fall into the hot mantle of the Earth. The soil underneath our homes, schools, and buildings helps to keep them upright.

Soil for hundreds of years has been used as a simple and cheap building material. Clay bricks or mud bricks can be made to create shacks. Mud has been used to create adobe homes or patch up spaces in between wood or brick structures.

You can probably think of at least 5 animals that live in the soil. Where would they live without the soil? For slimy organisms like the earthworm, the soil is the best environment for them since it is dark and damp.

Technology may provide us with lots of other things we need in our lives, but don't forget the natural resources you have around you. Trees may provide you with apples for an apple pie or oxygen for your morning run. Water is great to quench your thirst and to make sure you stay cool at the beach. Plants are important to help feed other organisms. And, the soil is crucial to allow us to live the way we have for thousands of years.

Activities

Explore more about these natural resources with some exciting hands-on activities.

#1 Building Muddy Bricks

Materials:

- Ice cube tray
- Dirt or sand
- Large mixing bowl
- Water
- Measuring cups

Procedure:

1. Measure about a half a cup of dirt and pour it into the mixing bowl.
2. Measure out about ⅔ cup of water and pour into the mixing bowl.
3. Mix the dirt and water together in the bowl.
4. Place the mud into the ice cube openings in the ice cube tray.
5. Let the mud dry for an hour.
6. Then start building!

What's happening?

When dirt is mixed with water it forms mud. Mud has been used for years to build houses or patch up openings between bricks. When the mud is made, it is easy to work with, but when it hardens it forms a brick that can be used to build things.

#2: Filter away!

Materials:

- Water
- 4 different types of soil (can be potting soil, sand, clay, and dirt)
- Filter paper
- Plastic funnel
- 9 Large clear plastic cups
- Cup holder with stand
- Food coloring (red, blue, yellow, and green)
- Knife or scissors (ask for adult help when using these)

Procedure:

1. With an adult's help, poke at least ten holes in each of the plastic cups.
2. Cut out a circular piece of filter paper.
3. Place the circular filter paper in the bottom of each cup.
4. Fill each cup about halfway with soil. One soil type per cup.
5. Sit each cup inside of the plastic funnel with the bottom of the cup resting inside of the funnel.
6. Place each cup into the cup holder and place an empty plastic cup underneath each. This cup will catch the water as it is filtered by the soil.
7. In a separate cup add about 3 cups of water and 5-10 drops of food coloring.
8. Pour the about ¾ of a cup of water solution into each of the cups with soil.
9. Let the water drain out of each cup for 30 minutes.
10. Observe the color of the water collected in each plastic cup. What does the water look like now?

11. Repeat steps 6 - 9 with different colored water mixtures.

What's happening?

Soil is a natural filter. There are small holes in the soil for water to move through, but some things get absorbed. The food coloring gets absorbed in the soil and the water that is collected may have changed colors. In some cases, the water changed colors as it interacted with the components in the soil.

#3: Quick, quick, quick!

Materials:

- Sugar (can be cubes or granulated)
- 2 clear glass cup
- Water (preferably cold water)
- Hot water
- Mixing spoon
- Tablespoon

Procedure:

1. Fill each glass cup with water. One should have cold water and another should have hot water. The cups should have an equal amount of water in each.
2. Place two tablespoons of sugar in the cold water and stir.
3. Repeat step 2 with the hot water. Which glass dissolved the sugar the fastest?

4. Continue to add one tablespoon of water to each mixture, slowly, and stirring each time. Which mixture took more sugar?

What's happening?

Both the cold water and the hot water dissolved the sugar, but one dissolved more. The hot water dissolves more sugar because the water particles are moving faster in the hot water and able to dissolve more than in the cold water. Think about this in nature. The oceans are able to dissolve more nutrients for the animals in the summertime than in the winter when the water is colder.

#4: Water's on the move!

Materials:

- 2 clear plastic cups
- Water
- 3 sheets of paper towel

Procedure:

1. Take the three sheets of paper towel and twist them to make a "paper towel rope".
2. Pour water in one of the plastic cups and sit the two cups side by side.
3. In the cup with water, put one end of the paper towel and drape the other end of the paper towel into the empty plastic cup. So, one end of the paper towel should be in the water and the other end should be in the empty cup without water.

4. Observe the cups for 30 minutes. What happens to the empty cup?

What's happening?

What is a fantastic substance! You may have noticed that the empty cup begin to fill with water. Cool, right? This is called capillary action, where water is able to "walk up" substances to go from one place to another. This is a great way for plants to transport water as it is absorbed in their roots and has to go up through the stem to the leaves.

#5: Colorful dying plants

Materials:

- 10-15 pieces of onion skins
- Large cooking pot
- Water
- Several large raw eggs
- Mixing spoon
- Cloth cut into squares (these should be large enough to wrap the eggs
- Rubber bands

Procedure:

1. Soak the cloth and the onion skin in lukewarm water.
2. Wrap the egg with onion skins until the egg is completely covered.
3. Place the egg inside of the cloth and close shut with the rubber band
4. Fill the cooking pot halfway with water and place the cloth-wrapped eggs into the pot.
5. Ask an adult to place the pot on the stove and boil the eggs for 20-30 minutes.

6. Let the pot cool for 30 minutes and remove the clothed-wrapped eggs.

7. Take off the rubber bands and look at your new dyed eggs!

What's happening?

Plants have special pigments within them that help them to absorb light so that they can go through photosynthesis to make their own food. These same pigments contain colors or dyes that can be used to die cloths or like what you saw eggs! Plants have been used for hundreds if years to make beautiful colors for fabrics and textiles.

Quiz

1. Name two things that rocks provide.
2. Without rocks, there would be no _____.
3. What are precious stones used for?
4. The Native Americans used obsidian to make _____.
5. Why do sculptors use rock instead of other materials like paper?
6. What is the most important substance on Earth?
7. True or False. Water is not involved in temperature regulation (like keeping you cool).
8. True or False. When water freezes, it sinks to the bottom of the ocean.
9. What is the importance of ice?
10. Water is needed to transport _____.
11. What do plants produce that humans and other animals need to survive?
12. True or False. In a food chain, plants are at the top.
13. True or False. Plants are also called the primary producers.
14. What would happen to the other animals in a food chain, if plants were eliminated?
15. Name three things we get from plants.
16. True or False. Maple syrup and rubber come from trees.
17. Name an herb and what it helps to cure.
18. Name two animals that have plant habitats.
19. Name one animal that has soil habitats.
20. Rocks, water, plants, and soil are all considered _____ resources.

Quiz Answers

1. Rocks can provide shelter, soil, art materials, and tools.
2. Without rocks, there would be no soil. Remember soil comes from sediment (or broken rock) mixed with dead matter like leaves and decaying/dead animals.
3. Precious stones are often used to make jewelry.
4. The Native Americans used obsidian to make arrowheads.
5. Sculptors use rock instead of other materials because rock will not fall apart easily. It will eventually erode but only after hundreds of years.
6. Water is the most important substance on Earth. All organisms need water to survive.
7. False. Water is involved in temperature regulation. Think about when you sweat. As you sweat, water leaves your body and evaporates. When it evaporates it takes the heat away from your body and helps you stay cool.
8. False. When water freezes, it rises or floats to the top of the ocean. This is very important because if ice sunk, the oceans may completely freeze, killing all the animals in the ocean.
9. Ice floats and in the winter the layer of ice that forms at the tops of oceans is able to insulate (warm) the water below it.
10. Water is needed to transport nutrients. This is true because water is the universal solvent, meaning it is able to dissolve most substances.
11. Plants produce oxygen which humans and other animals need to survive.
12. False. In a food chain, plants are at the bottom. This does not mean they are unimportant, instead the position at the bottom shows that they support or hold up the other organisms in the food chain.
13. True. Plants are also called the primary producers. This is because they are the first organisms in a food chain. They produce their own food and then are consumed or eaten by other animals in the food chain.
14. Without plants, the other animals would eventually die.
15. From plants we are able to get materials for clothing (cotton), food, oxygen to breathe, medicines, and building materials (wood or bamboo).
16. True. Maple syrup and rubber come from trees.
17. The daffodil is used to treat Alzheimer's and the Foxglove plant has been used since the 1500s to treat heart disease.
18. Answers may vary. In the section, the birds, squirrels, and snakes were given as examples of organisms that live in trees.
19. Answers may vary. In the section, the earthworm was named as an example of an organism that lives in the soil.
20. Rocks, water, plants, and soil are all considered environmental (or natural) resources.

Earth Science #4: Fossils

Fossils are a way that we can learn more about the past. Paleontologists study fossils and the types of life forms that existed millions of years ago. For some organisms that are extinct, like dinosaurs, fossils are the only way we can study them.

What are fossils? How are they formed?

Fossils are the remains of animals and plants and they have been found all over Earth. In order to form a fossil, the animal or plant has to be quickly buried immediately after death. This can be done by sinking into the mud, or being buried by a large sandstorm. Most of the animal will rot or decay, like the fur, skin, organs, and muscles. The harder parts of the animal like the bones and teeth will remain and will be covered with newly formed rock. It is important for the new layer of rock to form quickly so that the animal's remains are not washed away.

Eventually the chemicals that are released by the animals decaying body will cause the bones to remain hard materials of the animal to decompose. As the bone breaks down, minerals come in from the surrounding rock and form a rock impression where the existing bone was. This is what gives the fossil its shape, looking identical to the dead organism.

Material like trees can also form fossils through a process called petrification. In this process, hard and soft portions of a plant or animal are replaced with a special type of natural material called silica or calcite. This causes the wood to look more like rock.

Insects and pieces of plants can get trapped in tree sap and be petrified for millions of years. The tree sap is very sticky but over time can harden and form amber. This is a useful way to study the insects since it keeps them suspend in the amber and their body and parts stay together.

Not all organisms are able to form fossils. Most animals and plants that die decompose, or their remains are washed away. Only a very small percentage of organisms are captured in fossils. Scientists believe that less than 0.1% of all dinosaurs that once roamed the Earth are found in fossils.

What are the different types of fossils?

Each fossil is not created equal. In fact, there are five different types of fossils. They are: cast fossils, mold fossils, carbon film fossils, trace fossils, and preserved remains fossils. We'll look at each type, how their made, and what we can learn from them.

Cast Fossils

If you think of when you have heard the word "cast". If you have ever broken a bone, you may have had to wear a cast to cover the area. Similar to a cast you may have to wear, a cast fossil is a 3-D fossil. It is made by using a mold. A mold is formed when an animal or plant dies lands on rock or a soft material like clay or mud and remains there as it decays. The animal or plant leaves behind a mold or an impression. Over time, water, sediment, and other dissolved minerals like calcium come in and fill the mold. The sediment and minerals begin to come together and form rock, making a cast, or a 3-D image of the animal or plant. As we go on to the next type of fossil, the mold fossil, keep in mind that cast and mold fossils are opposite of each other. In other words, a cast is the opposite of a mold and a mold is the opposite of a cast.

Mold Fossils

If a cast is a 3-D version of the animal, then what is a mold? A mold only forms with animal remains. This is because the hard parts of the animal like the bones will get buried in sand or clay. Over time as the hard parts decay and dissolve they will leave behind an impression of the animal's shape. This is the mold. Mold fossils can sometimes be called impression fossils. Imagine taking a fork and pressing it into a piece of clay. What is left behind are the marks of the fork. This is similar to what happens when a mold fossil is formed. Mold fossils can provide some information about the animal, but because they are only formed from the hard parts of the animal, we do not learn as much as we could.

Carbon Film Fossils

Did you know that all living things have carbon within them? Yes, it is true. Carbon is considered to be one of the first elements on Earth and is within all of us. When an animal or plant dies and is immediately buried in sand, clay, or mud the carbon and other things within them begins to decompose. Over a long period of time, only the carbon will be left. Carbon takes a very long time to disappear. Scientists can study the leftover carbon and learn a little about the soft parts of the animal like the muscles, skin, and even the organs. Carbon film fossils can also be used to study plants and learn more about all parts of the plant including the plant's stem, roots, and leaves.

Trace Fossils

Have you ever left a footprint in the sand or the mud? If so, then you've left a trace fossil. Trace fossils can provide scientists with information about an organism's activities, how they traveled, how heavy they were, etc. The depth and size of the marking left has lots of information that scientists can study. But how does a footprint become a fossil? Eventually the footprint gets buried with layers of sediment and this sediment then turns into solid rock. The rock that results has the same shape and size as the footprint it covered.

Preserved Remains Fossils:

These fossils form when an animal or plant becomes trapped within a substance. Preserved fossils are commonly made from: amber, tar, or ice.

Amber, we talked about, is the solid form of sap from a tree. Insects can get stuck and die and are preserved for thousands, if not millions of years.

When an animal dies and is trapped in a tar pit, the tar eventually soaks into their body and stops the bones from breaking down. This preserves the hard parts of the animal for scientists to study.

Animals that lived in very cold environments may die and become frozen or enclosed in ice. They will stay frozen in the ice for millions of years and scientists can study lots about these animals. Ice keeps the organism intact and scientists can even study the hairs and nails of the animal thousands of years later!

How are fossils found?

Fossils have to be excavated or dug up from rock layers. Sedimentary rocks contain fossils. This is because when an animal or plant dies, it lies on top of a layer of sedimentary rock and is over time covered with the next layer of sedimentary rock. The layers of rock serve to encase or protect the decomposing plant or animal, leaving impressions of the animal or plant in the layers of rock above and below it. Fossils do not contain bones, but do keep their original shape. Since fossils are enclosed in rocks for thousands, if not millions of years, they have more characteristics in common with rocks.

How are fossils dated?

Scientists can use a technique called carbon dating. We know that all organisms have carbon within them and carbon takes about 5,500 years to decompose half of the carbon in an organism. Scientists have samples of very old organisms that they know the age of. When a fossil is found, they can compare the amount of carbon in the fossil to the samples and determine the age of the fossil. The less carbon in the fossil, the older it is. Remember carbon decays very slowly so if only a very small amount is left that means the fossil must have been created thousands, if not millions of years ago for there to be such small amounts of carbon remaining.

Fossils are our view into the past. Through the discovery and study of fossils over 1,000 dinosaurs have been found. The more fossils that are excavated the more we can learn about dinosaurs and other plants and animals. Finding fossils is not a new phenomenon. Many believe that even the Greeks and the Romans discovered and studied fossils hundreds of years ago. There are many more fossils still trapped under layers of rock and Earth that have yet to be discovered. We are even creating fossils today that scientist hundreds and thousands of years from now can study to learn more about our present day plant and animals.

Want to explore more with fossils? Try these hands-on science experiments and keep adding to your knowledge and understanding of fossils! As you work through these experiments test yourself and see if you can keep track of the different types of fossils that were discussed in this section.

Activities

#1: Ready, Set, Cast!

Materials:

- ¥Modeling clay and Plaster of Paris
- ¥plastic soda bottles
- ¥Plastic small toy dinosaurs (or sticks and leaves)
- ¥Large mixing bowl

Procedure:

- 1. Cut the plastic bottles into two-inch circles or rings.
- 2. Section off the clay into pieces that can easily fit into the plastic bottle rings, leaving ½ inch space at the top of the ring.
- 3. Smooth out the clay as much as possible.
- 4. Take the toy dinosaurs or other objects and press them into the clay for 30 seconds and then remove.
- 5. Mix the Plaster of Paris in the large mixing bowl. Only mix enough to pour into the plastic ring with the clay.
- 6. Pour the Plaster of Paris into the rings with the clay, filling it to the top of the ring.
- 7. Leave the plastic ring with the Plaster of Paris untouched for 30-45 minutes for it to completely harden.
- 8. Push the clay and the Plaster of Paris out of the ring.

What's happening?

In this experiment, you created a cast fossil. Cast fossils are made when an animal gets trapped in the soil or clay immediately after it dies and then they are covered with sedimentary rock. As the animal decays, the rock replaces the soft and hard parts of the animal's body, leaving a cast. The newly formed rock will take the shape of the animal.

#2: Make a good impression…

Materials:

- ¥Plaster of Paris
- ¥Paper cups (6 ounce size is best)
- ¥Plastic small toy dinosaurs (or sticks and leaves)
- ¥Large mixing bowl
- ¥Napkins or paper towels

Procedure:

- 1. Cut the tops off of the small paper cups, leaving about one inch of cup.
- 2. Mix the Plaster of Paris in the large mixing bowl.
- 3. Pour the Plaster of Paris into the paper cup sections.
- 4. Let the Plaster of Paris sit for three minutes, allowing it to slowly harden.
- 5. Take the two dinosaurs or other object and firmly press it into the Plaster of Paris. Be sure not to twist or turn the object. Press firmly down, and let the object remain in the Plaster of Paris for 5 minutes.
- 6. Slowly and carefully remove the object from the cup.
- 7. Leave the cup with the Plaster of Paris untouched for 30-45 minutes for it to completely harden.
- 8. Peel the cup from around the Plaster of Paris.

What's happening?

You've just made a mold fossil. Mold fossils occur when the animal's remains fall on newly formed rock and make an impression in the rock. The other kind of fossil is a cast fossil. Mold fossils provide a 2-D representation of the animal and do not provide as much information as a cast fossil. Fossils of any kind do give scientists an inside view into the life of prehistoric plants and animals.

#3: The bouncy, bouncy egg

Materials:

- ¥ Vinegar
- ¥ Clear glass jar with lid
- ¥ Raw egg

Procedure:

1. Fill the glass jar with vinegar within an inch of the top of the jar.
2. Carefully place the egg in the jar.
3. Put the lid on the glass jar.
4. Leave the egg in the jar for at least 4 days, until the shell has disappeared.
5. Gently pour out the vinegar.
6. Feel the egg, gently squeezing it.

What's happening?

The egg's shell disappeared! The egg's shell is made up of calcium like our bones. When an animal dies they slowly decompose. The soft parts like the organs, skin, and muscles degrade first. Eventually the bones and harder portions of the animal also degrade leaving behind nothing or a fossil if the animal has decomposed on rock. The vinegar is able to eat through the egg's shell, leaving the soft lining of the egg. If you were to leave the egg for weeks, it would completely decompose, leaving no trace of the egg.

#4: Digging for fossils

Note: This experiment requires **adult supervision**.

Materials:

- ¥Chocolate chips (at least 3 cups)
- ¥Metal mixing spoon
- ¥Microwave or cooking pot with stove
- ¥Styrofoam or paper cups
- ¥Gummy worms
- ¥Refrigerator

Procedure:

- 1. Melt 2 cups of chocolate using the microwave or a cooking pot. Make sure to stir the chocolate every 30-40 seconds to prevent burning. Be very careful handling this as the chocolate will be very hot and can cause burns.
- 2. Slowly and carefully pour the chocolate into the paper cups. Fill the paper cup about halfway.
- 3. Place the gummy worm in the chocolate.
- 4. Fill the rest of the cup with chocolate completely covering the gummy worm.
- 5. Place the paper cup in the refrigerator for 45-60 minutes.
- 6. Peel the paper cup from around the chocolate and dig for your gummy worm!

What's happening?

Remember sedimentary rock forms fossils. When an animal dies and falls on already formed rock, new rock forms on top of the animal, encasing it in two layers of rock. This is what you did with your gummy worm. The old rock was the chocolate you poured into the cup in the beginning, and the new rock was the chocolate you poured over the gummy worm. The worm was encased or completely covered with chocolate like an animal is completely covered by rock when a fossil forms.

#5: Under great pressure...

Materials:

- ¥3 slices of bread
- ¥Gummy worms or gummy bears
- ¥Three to four heavy books
- ¥Paper towels

Procedure:

- 1. Place one slice of bread on a paper towel.
- 2. Place a few gummy worms/bears on top of the bread.
- 3. Place another slice of bread and more gummy worms/bears on that layer.
- 4. Place the final layer of bread on the top.
- 5. Wrap the entire bread "structure" in a paper towel.
- 6. Place the paper towel with the bread on top of a book and place several books on top of it.
- 7. Press firmly down on the top books for 2 minutes.
- 8. Leave the books on top of the paper towel overnight.
- 9. Remove the books and open the paper towel to examine the bread and gummy worms.

What's happening?

Fossils are created over time and under lots and lots of pressure. What did the bread mixture look like after it had been under the pressure of the books for several hours? When a fossil forms, the animal's remains are also crushed under the layers of new rock that form.

Quiz

1.) Who studies rocks?

2.) What can we learn from fossils?

3.) True or False. Most organisms form fossils.

4.) How is petrified wood made?

5.) Hardened tree sap is called _____.

6.) How are fossils made?

7.) True or False. Fossils can only be found in the desert.

8.) True or False. Fossils will have the bones of the animal.

9.) Fossils have to be _____.

10.) What type of rock makes fossils?

11.) How are fossils dated?

12.) What are the five types of fossils?

13.) True or False. Scientists can learn more from carbon film fossils than from preserved remains.

14.) Name two types of substances that can create preserved remain fossils.

15.) What is the difference between a cast fossil and a mold fossil?

16.) All organisms have _____ within them.

17.) True or False. Mold fossils are the same as cast fossils.

18.) A footprint is an example of a _____ fossil.

19.) In which type of fossil can the hairs and nails of the organism be studied?

20.) Why would a plant mold fossil not exist?

Quiz Answers

1.) Paleontologists study fossils.

2.) Fossils give us a look into the past. They are very helpful in studying plants and animals that are extinct.

3.) False. Most organisms do not form fossils. Instead, when they die, they are decomposed and their remains are washed away.

4.) Petrified wood is made when minerals seep into the cracks of the wood and replace most of the wood material with rock.

5.) Hardened tree sap is called amber. Tree sap is very sticky and can cover an insect and keep it persevered for thousands of years.

6.) Fossils are made when an organism dies and is immediately covered by rock. The rock layers (above and below) keep the organism in place. As the hard material like bone decomposes over hundreds of years, it leaves an impression behind in the fossil.

7.) False. Fossils have been found all over the world, on each continent.

8.) False. Fossils will have the same shape of the animal, but there will be no bone material remaining.

9.) Fossils have to be excavated or dug up. They are often buried under several layers of rock.

10.) Sedimentary rocks make fossils.

11.) Fossils can be dated using a process called carbon dating. Scientists compare the amount of carbon in the fossil with the amount of carbon in other fossils to see how old the fossil is.

12.) The five types of fossils are: cast fossils, mold fossils, carbon film fossils, trace fossils, and preserved remains fossils.

13.) False. Scientists can learn more from carbon film fossils than from preserved remains. Preserved remains fossils have the animal intact and allow scientist to study the entire animal. Carbon film fossils are only able to study the animal based on the carbon that remains. Most of the animal would have decomposed by the time scientists find the fossil.

14.) Preserved remains fossils can be made using amber, tar, or ice.

15.) A cast fossil is a 3-D representation of the animal whereas a mold fossil is just a 2-D version similar to just an impression fossil.

16.) All organisms have carbon within them.

17.) False. Mold fossils are the opposite of cast fossils.

18.) A footprint is an example of a trace fossil.

19.) In a preserved remains fossil encased in ice the hairs and nails of the organism can be studied thousands of years later.

20.) Mold fossils are made from the hard parts of an organism, like the bones. Plants do not have bones and would not have any hard parts to form a mold fossil.

Made in the USA
Lexington, KY
05 September 2016